HOW TO EAT *a* PEACH

menus, stories, and places

DIANA HENRY

MITCHELL BEAZLEY

For Joss Herd, with love

An Hachette UK Company
www.hachette.co.uk

First published in Great Britain in 2018 by Mitchell Beazley,
a division of Octopus Publishing Group Ltd
Carmelite House, 50 Victoria Embankment
London EC4Y 0DZ
www.octopusbooks.co.uk

Distributed in the US by Hachette Book Group
1290 Avenue of the Americas
4th and 5th Floors, New York, NY 10104

Distributed in Canada by Canadian Manda Group
664 Annette St., Toronto, Ontario, Canada M6S 2C8

ISBN 978 1 78472 411 5
Printed and bound in China
10 9 8 7 6 5 4 3

Group Publishing Director: Denise Bates
Creative Director: Jonathan Christie
Photographer: Laura Edwards
Photographic Assistant: Kendal Noctor
Design and Art Direction: Miranda Harvey
Editor: Lucy Bannell
Home Economist and Food Stylist: Joss Herd
Assistant Home Economists: India Whiley Morton
and Camilla Baynham
Senior Production Manager: Katherine Hockley

Diana Henry tests all her recipes in a convection oven.
Please refer to your oven manufacturer's instruction
booklet if not working with a convection oven.

contents

introduction

When I was sixteen I started to keep a book of menus, a school exercise book I'd carefully covered in wrapping paper. This was an odd obsession, because I didn't cook most of the menus I created; I would've needed a restaurant to get through them all. The pleasure was in putting the menus together, thinking long and hard about what dishes worked.

I still have the book. Most of the meals are simple: cucumber salad with dill and sour cream, goulash, baked autumn fruit; crudités (the kind I'd had in France), *poulet bonne femme, galette aux pommes.* There aren't any dishes from some of the cuisines I now love—Middle Eastern or Vietnamese, for example— but there are a few old-fashioned, embarrassingly complicated menus I wouldn't dream of attempting these days: buckwheat blinis with warm melted butter, sour cream, and smoked salmon; guinea fowl breasts in pastry with mushrooms duxelles and Madeira sauce; Grand Marnier soufflé. I did actually cook this. Was I mad?

My parents didn't have dinner parties. They gave parties, though. These weren't formal, and you were invited verbally ("Come on over. We're having a few people in.") They were about good *craic*, drinking Bushmills whiskey and Vat 69, and dancing to Nancy Sinatra. My mum prepared wonderful food, dishes that would be laid out, buffet-style, on the big dining table. She thought about what worked together. She was going to cooking classes (she was always going to cooking classes) and made dishes that were, for that time, exotic: braised pork with bell peppers and paprika; 'slaw with caraway seeds; an "Austrian" coffee cake that was soaked in booze. Some of the recipes came from her classes, others from the Cordon Bleu magazines she was collecting (and which I pored over at night until my eyes hurt). From these parties, as well as from the pages of Cordon Bleu, I got the idea that having people over to eat wasn't just about food, but about creating an event, an atmosphere.

I gave my first "dinner party" soon after I started keeping my menu book. My school friends were bemused by the candlelit room (I'd gone over the top). "Are we going to celebrate mass?" one asked. And they didn't quite get the pineapple water ice ("What *is* this?") but I continued, undaunted. I loved "having people over" but, even more, I loved putting a menu together.

Years later I discovered Alice Waters's *Chez Panisse Menu Cookbook*, a thrill for the menu fanatic. The book contains recipes, of course, but it's also an archive of menus served at Chez Panisse restaurant in Berkeley, California. The place was unusual, especially for that time, in that it offered only set menus.

Set menus were and are common in France but, when Alice started serving them in the 1970s, they were not the norm either in America or Britain. As Chez Panisse was run mostly by people who weren't trained chefs, it made sense to offer the same food to everyone—they couldn't have managed a big à la carte menu—and I was fascinated by the meals they'd put together. It wasn't restauranty; it was like the food that a very good and thoughtful home cook would make. When I moved to London in the mid-1980s, I soon learned that Clarke's restaurant—owned and run by Sally Clarke, who had worked at Chez Panisse—also offered set menus. I used to get on the subway on a Monday night to go and see what Sally had planned for the week. I'd stand there, sometimes in the rain, with a little flashlight, writing down her menus in a notebook. I rarely ate at Clarke's (I was in my first job and it was expensive), but I felt as if I ate there all the time.

Composing a menu is still my favorite bit of cooking. I don't invite people over and then wonder what I'll cook. I come up with a menu and then consider who would like to eat it.

Why did I decide to write a whole book of menus, when people can compose their own? Because I get more questions about menus than about anything else. Friday nights and Saturday mornings bring endless phone calls and texts. Friends, preparing meals for Saturday night, have decided on a main course but don't know what to have for dessert (desserts are nearly always an afterthought), and everybody wants a "quick" appetizer. "Will these dishes work together?" is something I'm always being asked.

There are some practical "rules" about menus, though they're open to being bent, even completely broken. You'll pick up more throughout the book, but here are my basic guidelines. Ideally, no more than two courses should be cooked at the last minute, otherwise you'll be stressed. (This rule can be dispensed with if you are one of those cooks who can deep-fry while making sparkling conversation with twelve people. I am not one of those cooks.)

A meal shouldn't be too rich: cream should only appear in one course (though you can always have it with dessert). It's not ideal to repeat ingredients. In general, if I start with fish, it won't appear again (though I break this "rule," as you'll see). Consider color, texture, and temperature and—it almost goes without saying—eat seasonally.

Make sure your guests aren't going to be full by the end of the first course (the Australian restaurateur Gay Bilson has written that the appetite should be piqued as you eat, rather than sated).

Most of the menus in this book contain three courses, though some have five, while others are made up of dishes that are all served at the same time. I love mezze and tapas—you get to taste so many different things—and I understand the modern desire for "small plates," but I still cleave, mostly, to the notion of a meal that progresses from one course to the next, however recent, in historical terms, that idea is.

I often start meals with a salad, because it's such an "appetite-opening" way to begin, but you don't need an "appetizer" at all. You can always begin with things guests can pick at: radishes, charcuterie, olives.

Radishes with quail eggs and tapenade—or just with good bread, butter, and salt—is my go-to "opener." Then there are "crudités." These are not the sorry flaccid raw-vegetables-plus-dip that you see in supermarkets, but the small array of vegetable salads—*carrottes rapées*, *lentilles en salade*, leeks vinaigrette—that the French serve.

A main course doesn't have to be a hunk of protein with side dishes; it can be about the same size as the appetizer, and it doesn't have to be meat- or fish-based at all. The vegetarian menus in the book are there quite by accident, not because I tried to include vegetarian-friendly options. Soup is hard to fit into any dinner (it's just too filling), but lunch can be built on it. I love a plain green salad after the main course and, though it only appears once in this book, you can slot them into any meal. It was one of the things I came to appreciate on my first trip to France and became almost my favorite part of every meal; it was cleansing and refreshing and provided a kind of interlude. But the greens have to be good, and good greens don't come pre-washed in a bag. Buy proper lettuce in heads; depending on the variety it will keep in the fridge for days (especially curly endive (frisée), Belgian endive, and romaine). Wash what you need, dry the leaves thoroughly, and make a good vinaigrette, by which I mean taste it as you make it. There are agreed general proportions for vinaigrette, of course, but they will vary for each one you make, depending on the vinegar and the oil you are using, as well as the leaves you are dressing.

Dessert can be dropped in favor of cheese—and remember that one good cheese is better than four average pieces—a perfectly ripe bit of fruit, or a glass of dessert wine. I prefer fruit desserts, though sometimes I long for something chocolatey and slightly bitter. There are several types of ice cream in this book, because you can fuse flavors in them. This is a thoughtful way to end a meal. An ice cream can combine grapefruit and basil, chocolate and luscious sweet Pedro Ximénez, bourbon, maple syrup, and apples. Because cookbooks only feature dishes that the author likes, there are no cheesecakes or meringues. I don't think they have a place at the end of a meal (they're too sweet and too heavy).

You don't always have to serve bread—guests can overdo it and fill themselves up—but it's important with mezze-type meals, as they generally contain dishes that need to be scooped up. If you're going to have bread, serve good stuff, and good butter, too.

There are people more qualified than I who can advise on what wines to serve with what foods, but I've suggested special drinks. A wintry kir made with red wine and cassis (it's called a "communard"), home-made bergamot syrup mixed with sparkling white wine; these make a meal special, and particular to you.

This book might have started out as a way to give practical advice, but it ended up being about place, too. There is poetry in menus. They can transport you to the Breton coast, or to a Saturday night in Manhattan; they are short stories. I didn't realize, though, until I started to put the menus for this book together, just how important the conjuring-up of place through food is to me. It's one of the reasons I cook. I think this is because I grew up in Northern Ireland. I didn't go abroad until I was fifteen, when

I traveled to France on my own, on an exchange trip. There were very few destinations you could fly to directly from Belfast. You generally had to go via London, which meant that traveling was expensive. If you wanted to go places, you had to do it in your head—via books—or by cooking the food of other countries.

When I did start to travel, everywhere seemed very intense: Spain (raw light, heat, olive oil, the smell of tobacco) was very Spanish; New York really did have "WALK/DON'T WALK" signs; Morocco felt almost biblical. I love traveling, but I'm quite timid. I feel difference very keenly. I notice everything and the sense of a place stays with me. Part of my cooking is about revisiting places, and even expressing feelings about particular places.

I have tried, throughout this book, to suggest alternatives to dishes, so that you can make the menus easier to achieve, if you need to. Obviously you can slot in ideas of your own, too. Although I wanted to offer a book of considered meals, I didn't intend them to be set in stone. Also, feel free to use the recipes independently because there are dishes in here that make a fine Friday night supper, with neither appetizer nor dessert.

The term "entertaining" makes me think of hostess trollies and instructions on how to plump up your cushions. I really don't do "entertaining." I just have friends over. Often I serve dinner (or supper, or whatever you want to call it) in the midst of a mess, otherwise I wouldn't see friends at all. I'm happy to put a roasting pan on the table and ask someone else to carve (I am terrible at carving). I don't think you should kill yourself over dinner, but at the same time I do like all the stuff that goes with it: table linen, plates, old cutlery. I have spent a lifetime gathering this up and I like spending time on it, when I can. Having people over to eat is about food…and yet it isn't. Meals, no matter how simple, are made better by small things: flowers, candles, a pitcher of water. They're also made bad by small things: salami served in the plastic package in which it comes, poor bread. I don't like the suggestion—prevalent these days—that cooking is all about "lifestyle." I think it's about taking care of the small, seemingly unimportant things.

The idea for this book came to me years ago; nearly all of my books have been in my head for a long time. In a single moment I realized how much other people, when cooking, care about these small things. At a restaurant in Italy (on my first trip there), the diners at the next table didn't have a fancy dessert, they just had a bowl of peaches and a bottle of cold Moscato. Everyone sliced their peach and dropped it into the wine. After a while they drank the wine—now imbued with the flavor of the peach—and ate the peach slices, which now tasted of the wine. This was not a complicated dish, but it was a lovely way to end a meal—seasonal, straightforward, caring, even a little magical—and it illustrated an approach to food and cooking that I already understood but hadn't yet articulated. I've never forgotten this. More than a memory, those peaches became a symbol of what good food is all about.

spring and summer

cider and gitanes

falling in love with france

kir breton

leeks with breton vinaigrette | rillettes

mouclade

crêpes *dentelles* with sautéed apples & caramel

Dark, flat sheets of cloud hung in the sky above me. By the time I got to Daniel's they belched rain, and I could hear the snarl of thunder. Daniel lived in a poor bit of Bordeaux, in an old apartment with his family, an angry father who swore through every meal, his birdlike grandma, with her floral house-coats and heavily penciled eyebrows, and his large, silent grandpa who never said anything, except to ask for the salt. I was working as an *au pair* at a small family-run zoo outside Bordeaux. Daniel was my boyfriend and the zoo-keeper. I often had supper at his place. On this stormy day the film star Romy Schneider had died. Grandma was in tears. In honor of Romy, a bit more money than usual had been spent, there was *oeufs mayo* and leeks vinaigrette, a hunk of beef, pot-roasted with tomatoes and carrots and cut into soft slices, salad, and Roquefort. The bathroom in that apartment was housed in a few sheets of corrugated iron and had a rickety door; it was a demarcation rather than a room. The family was not well off, and yet food was always prepared with care. Grandma continued to sob, looking through her Romy Schneider cuttings, and we quietly ate baked pears.

My time in Bordeaux was my second experience of France. The first was an exchange trip, when I was fifteen. The parents in my host family both worked, but every day culminated in a good dinner. The mother would arrive home with fresh pizza dough, ready to be punched down, finished with a home-made topping and baked; or a friend would turn up for supper with an apricot tart she'd made on her afternoon off. Cooking was even more important when we went for a month to the father's home village (tiny Lamothe-en-Blaisy, though they called it Lamothe-en-Paradis and it was, indeed, paradise). Every day revolved around the preparation of meals. Clothilde, my counterpart, would start thinking about what to cook for lunch as soon as we'd finished breakfast. Would we do brochettes of lamb? What herb would we put in the vinaigrette today? Salad greens were carefully washed, then swung in a metal basket outside (the drier the greens, the better the vinaigrette would cling to them). Provisions were delivered in various vans, the cheesemongers and greengrocers negotiating the dirt tracks that wound between the houses. You could smell the mobile *fromagerie* before it had parked. I was astonished that the greengrocer sold summer fruits not in paper bags or small baskets, as in Great Britain, but in palettes. At home my mum counted out strawberries, dividing them equally among me and my siblings; in France there were glistening tarts piled high with raspberries and people bought stone fruits by the tray.

Clothilde and I spent afternoons at her grandma's going through ancient copies of *Elle*, marking up the dishes we wanted to try. Grandma taught me how to make *tarte aux pommes* with a filling of eggs and crème fraîche; Clothilde's brother showed me how to make perfect crêpes. I loved supper at their aunt's house. Meals there always began with crudités and charcuterie. This array, accompanied by baguette with a crust that shattered when you broke it, seemed the best way to start any meal, and Paris-Brest, which was often purchased, the best way to end it. (My love for that caused shameful transgressions. It was kept in the sideboard, under a cloth, and I would steal slivers between lunch and dinner. When I got caught red-handed, the father smiled, "*C'est bon le gateau, hé Diana?*")

Back at home, my dream of France was nurtured, fed by films—Truffaut, Chabrol, and especially those of Eric Rohmer (I liked dramas in which nothing happened, except talking and looking and longing)—books, and cooking. For years, my notebook of "dishes to cook" was full of French regional classics, and many of my fantasy meals were served on checkered tablecloths with a Jacques Brel soundtrack. In my twenties, I covered almost the entire country with Patricia Wells's *Food Lover's Guide to France* as my companion. I read about places I couldn't afford, or that were so out of the way I would never find them. The book sent me to a farm in Normandy where they made their own hard cider and served it with platters of ham and eggs, and to a hotel with a cupboard housing fifty kinds of jam. In a small inn on the French-Swiss border—where the air smelled of cool grass—I had a cloud of cheese soufflé and perfectly cooked trout for dinner, then couldn't sleep because of the tinkling of cowbells (I lay in the dark, thinking how wonderful it was not to be able to sleep because of the *sound of cowbells*).

I could have chosen a meal from any bit of France, but the most accessible areas, once I was living in London, were Normandy and Brittany and, later, the coast by La Rochelle. For years, I went to the French seaside at Easter. A trip to Normandy always meant a meal at Les Vapeurs in Trouville, an Art Deco brasserie with paper tablecloths, swift, skinny waiters, and teetering towers of *fruits de mer* on avalanches of crushed ice. I couldn't afford the platters then, but I was happy with a pot of mussels cooked in hard cider, enriched with Normandy cream. Brittany meant buckwheat crêpes, more hard cider, and a wilder coastline. It's a place set apart from the rest of France, harsh and no-nonsense, less romantic. Lunch there was oysters and sourdough from a stand on the roadside, supper a roll-your-sleeves-up affair where you tucked into shrimp and crab claws. The salty tang of seaweed and the aroma of caramelized sugar—from mobile *crêperies*—hung in the air.

There was a time when good food meant French food. To me it still does, though now you have to know where to find it. In France, as elsewhere, food has become industrialized. The country has lost its influence, partly because, in the area of haute cuisine, Spain flexed its muscles, then the Nordic countries, though Western chefs still rely on French technique more than any other. My kitchen, like that of many cooks, is now full of Middle Eastern grains and Asian spices. Travel has opened doors. Interest in food has increased, but at the same time we take the old and the familiar for granted; there's a tendency to love the new, whatever is "now." Classic French food is both simple and complex. The dishes appear to be easy, but you have to pay attention. Dishes have harmony and what the French call *volupté*, meaning they please the senses. A lot of modern food, in contrast, can be cerebral and austere; the elements sit on the plate but don't come together. A good friend, who is a restaurant critic, often says, "Whatever happened to deliciousness?" Then we daydream about a perfectly dressed green salad, cassoulet, and tarte Tatin.

Even though I'd already learned a lot in our kitchen at home in Northern Ireland, France was the first place that showed me the joy that cooking could bring me, both in the process and in the dishes I could put on the table. It pretty much made me a cook. So France is where we're going first.

kir breton

Kirs are usually made with crème de cassis and, traditionally, Bourgogne Aligoté (a white Burgundy), but *kirs Bretons*—and also *kirs Normands*—are made with hard cider. Just put a drop of crème de cassis in the bottom of each glass and top it off with a dry hard cider…preferably from Brittany or Normandy, obviously.

leeks with breton vinaigrette

Leeks vinaigrette was one of the dishes that made me fall in love with French food; I ate it on my first trip to France when I went there on an exchange trip. Most people can make leeks vinaigrette without a recipe, but the dressing here, which I tried while on vacation in Brittany, goes beyond the standard and is worth knowing. I usually serve this with the other bits and pieces that make up the French array of dishes they describe (rather modestly) as crudités: radishes, hard-boiled eggs, charcuterie, sometimes other vegetable dishes such as *carrottes rapées* and *lentilles en salade*.

serves 4

1 scant tablespoon white wine vinegar, or to taste

¼ teaspoon Dijon mustard, or to taste

pinch of ground allspice

sea salt flakes and freshly ground black pepper

½ cup extra virgin olive oil

good pinch of superfine sugar

1½ tablespoons capers, rinsed and patted dry

½ tablespoon very finely chopped shallot

1 tablespoon finely chopped flat-leaf parsley leaves

½ tablespoon each finely chopped chervil leaves and chives

6 medium leeks

Make the vinaigrette by mixing together the white wine vinegar, Dijon mustard, and allspice with some salt and pepper in a small bowl.

Whisk in the extra virgin olive oil with a fork. Add the sugar, capers, shallot, and herbs and taste for seasoning and balance (you might need a little more vinegar or mustard). It's good to make this about 30 minutes in advance, so that the flavors can meld.

Remove the tough outer leaves from the leeks and discard them. Slice off the tufty bit on the base of each leek, and also the dark green tops. Cut the leeks into 1½-inch pieces. Wash them really well, making sure that you get rid of any grit or soil between the layers. Steam over boiling water—this way the leeks don't become too "wet"—for 4 to 6 minutes. They should be completely tender right through (test with the tip of a sharp knife).

As soon as they're done, place them on a clean dish cloth and gently pat to soak up the excess moisture; the dressing clings to the leeks much better if they're not wet. Immediately put them into a serving bowl and, while they're still hot, dress them with the vinaigrette. Taste to check the seasoning, then serve warm or at room temperature.

rillettes

Homemade rillettes usually taste better than purchased (at least when you're not in France). They do take time, though not a lot of effort, and this should be an easy meal, so buy the rillettes if you prefer. To render pork fat, cut the fat into cubes, melt it in a heavy saucepan over low heat, then strain the resulting liquid fat through a sieve. This recipe makes more than you need; half the quantity will feed four people and the rest, well sealed with fat, will last for up to four months in the fridge. Halve the quantities if you prefer, but be warned that it's better to make rillettes in large quantities, otherwise it tends to get dry while cooking, so I would recommend making this larger amount.

makes about 2¼lb

1lb 2oz boneless pork shoulder

1lb 2oz boneless pork belly, rind removed

¾lb rendered pork fat (see recipe introduction), or good-quality store-bought lard

6 thyme sprigs

3 bay leaves

4 cloves

generous pinch of ground allspice

generous grating of nutmeg

plenty of sea salt flakes and freshly ground black pepper

Cut the pork shoulder into strips about ¾ inch across, along the grain of the meat. Cut the belly into slices about ½ inch thick. Put the fat and ½ cup of water into a broad, heavy saucepan and set it over very low heat. Add all the meat. Tie the thyme, bay leaves, and cloves in a square of cheesecloth and add this to the pot. Cook over very low heat so the liquid just quivers, not bubbles, for about 4 hours. The meat shouldn't brown, just poach, and must always be covered with fat. Make sure it doesn't stick to the pan, and turn it over from time to time. Its ready when it is completely tender and feels as if you can gently pull it apart.

Once the meat has cooled a bit, remove the spice and herb bag and shred the meat in the pan, pulling it apart with 2 forks. It should break down into rough, soft strands. Strain the meat through a colander over a bowl to collect the fat. Put the meat into another bowl and add the allspice, nutmeg, and some salt and pepper; be generous, you need to season well to make good rillettes. Add enough of the fat to make a creamy mixture, and reserve the rest.

Put the mixture into bowls—or pack it into jars with no air pockets, if you want to keep it for longer—cover with parchment paper that you've rubbed with pork fat and let cool completely; it will firm up a bit. Melt some of the reserved pork fat and pour it over the tops to form a seal. Put the papers back on top and put in the fridge.

The rillettes taste better after a couple of days, though I tend to eat some right away. If you pack it in jars with no air pockets and cover with ¼ inch of fat, it should last in the fridge for about 4 months. Once you've broken the protective layer of fat, eat within 5 days.

mouclade

Mouclade is eaten in and around La Rochelle, on the west coast of France. There are different versions, but the characteristic ingredient is curry powder. The dish, when you include saffron as well, has a lovely golden color.

serves 4

good pinch of saffron threads

4½lb mussels

2 tablespoons unsalted butter

1 small onion, finely chopped

2 garlic cloves, crushed

¾ teaspoon curry powder

¼ cup brandy

2 teaspoons all-purpose flour

scant 1 cup dry white wine

scant 1 cup heavy cream

sea salt flakes and freshly ground black pepper

generous handful of flat-leaf parsley leaves, finely chopped

Put the saffron in a small bowl and add ⅓ cup boiling water. Let steep for 30 minutes.

Clean the mussels, removing any beards and barnacles (scrape the latter off with a table knife) and washing the shells. Tap each against the sink as you go and discard any that remain open and don't close.

Melt the butter in a pan and gently sauté the onion until soft but not colored. Add the garlic and curry powder and cook for another 2 minutes to release the curry's fragrance. Add the brandy and let it boil until it has reduced to a couple of tablespoons. Reduce the heat, then stir in the flour, mixing well until everything is smooth. Cook for a minute, then take the pan off the heat and gradually add the saffron and its water, stirring as you do so. Set aside.

Put the wine and the mussels into a large saucepan and cover. Cook over medium-high heat for about 4 minutes, shaking the pan from time to time, until the mussels have opened. Strain the mussels (use a large colander), collecting their liquor in a bowl underneath. Discard any mussels that haven't opened and put the rest back into the saucepan. Cover to keep warm.

Strain the pot liquor through a sieve lined with cheesecloth—you need to get rid of any sand or grit—and gently reheat the saffron sauce you were making earlier. Gradually add the strained pot liquor, stirring as you do so, then bring the sauce to a boil and simmer for about 3 minutes. Add the cream and simmer for a further 4 minutes until it has reduced and the sauce is a little thicker. Taste for seasoning and stir in the parsley.

Put the mussels in a large warmed serving bowl—or keep them in the saucepan in which they were cooked, if you prefer—pour the sauce over them, and serve immediately.

crêpes *dentelles* with sautéed apples & caramel

The word *dentelles* means "lace" and refers to the fine, delicate edges of these crêpes. Making them well requires a few tricks, though they're easy to master: quickly tilt the pan so that the batter thinly coats the bottom, pour off the excess every time you add more batter, adjust the heat as necessary, and be careful not to add too much butter. You need a well-seasoned skillet that has become nonstick through wear, or a good nonstick skillet. The first pancake is always a dud, so don't worry. I was taught to make these by my first French boyfriend. He was called Christophe. I was fifteen. So, for me, this is more than just a recipe.

serves 4

for the crêpes
1 cup all-purpose flour
2½ tablespoons superfine sugar
pinch of sea salt flakes
1¼ cups whole milk
1 medium egg, plus 1 egg yolk
2 tablespoons unsalted butter, melted, plus more to cook
crème fraîche, to serve

for the caramel
3½ tablespoons unsalted butter
½ cup heavy cream
½ cup soft light brown sugar, packed
½ teaspoon sea salt flakes
¼ teaspoon vanilla extract

for the apples
2 tart apples, peeled, halved, and cored
3½ tablespoons unsalted butter
3½ tablespoons superfine sugar

Sift the flour, sugar, and salt into a bowl and make a well in the center. In a bowl, beat the milk, egg, and egg yolk with ½ cup of water and gradually whisk this into the well, until smooth. Stir in the melted butter, cover, and let stand for 1 hour. (Or make this in a blender. Blend for 1 minute, scrape down the sides, then blend for 5 seconds.)

Meanwhile, to make the caramel, put the butter in a large saucepan (the sauce will bubble a lot and you need room for that) and melt it over medium heat. Add the cream, sugar, and salt and bring to a boil, stirring to help the sugar dissolve. Reduce the heat and simmer for 10 minutes, whisking from time to time. Add the vanilla.

Cut the apples into thin wedges, about ¼ inch at the thickest part, and heat the butter in a skillet. Don't crowd the skillet or the apples will steam instead of fry. Sauté on both sides until golden (they can still be a little firm in the middle). Sprinkle with the sugar and cook over medium heat until a little caramelized (about 3 minutes). Lay the apples on a plate in a single layer; if they're on top of each other they continue to cook and can lose their nice sugar-toasted edges.

Melt a very small piece of butter in a well-seasoned or nonstick skillet and swirl it, just to coat the pan. Ladle in batter—again just enough to thinly coat—quickly swirl it, and pour off any excess (these crêpes need to be really thin). Cook over medium heat until golden underneath, then flip with a metal spatula and cook the other side. Add small amounts of butter as needed, but never too much. If the pan gets too hot and you burn the butter, wipe it out and start again. Keep the crêpes in a pile in a low oven until you've cooked them all.

Serve the crêpes with the apples and caramel—if you've made the sauce in advance, gently reheat it if you like—and crème fraîche.

constant cravings

hot, sour, salty, sweet

galloping horses

stir-fried shrimp with sugar snaps, basil, chile & lime

korean cucumber salad (*oi muchim*)

braised pork with ginger & star anise

jenny's sago *gula melaka*

Some foods nag at me—the way a song plays insistently in your head—until I can eat them. And these cravings aren't just for one dish, but for a mixture of tastes, usually the fresh, hot, sour, salty, sweet flavors of southeastern Asia, China, Korea, and Japan. Chiles, pickled ginger, fish sauce, limes, and palm sugar all temporarily sate a longing that never goes away. I am no expert in any of these cuisines, but I eat them all, mixing dishes in a way that would horrify some (forgive me, purists, I am helpless).

With this menu, serve the shrimp, pork, and cucumber salad together, with rice, of course.

galloping horses

My version of a Thai classic. Serve it before you sit down to eat, but give out napkins: things can get messy.

serves 6

1 scant cup peanut oil

½ cup finely sliced shallots

1¼oz garlic (about 1 small head), finely sliced

3½oz ground chicken

3½oz raw shelled shrimp, vein removed, very finely chopped

¼ cup palm sugar, to taste

3 tablespoons fish sauce, to taste

juice of 1 lime, to taste

¼ cup roasted unsalted peanuts, coarsely crushed

½ small pineapple, peeled and cored

2 red Thai chiles, halved, seeded, and very finely sliced

2 Kaffir lime leaves, very finely sliced

⅓ cup cilantro leaves

for the garlic and cilantro paste
⅓ cup cilantro, coarsely chopped

4 garlic cloves, coarsely chopped

¼ teaspoon white peppercorns

Heat the oil in a small saucepan and, when it quivers, add the shallots and cook until dark gold, turning them over every so often. Strain through a mesh strainer, reserving the oil, and spread them on paper towels. Now heat 2 tablespoons of the reserved oil in a skillet and cook the garlic over medium heat until golden. Transfer to the paper towels.

Heat another 1 tablespoon of the oil in a wok and quickly fry the chicken, making sure it doesn't clump together. Transfer to a bowl. Repeat with the shrimp, adding a little more oil if needed. Add to the chicken.

For the cilantro and garlic paste, pound the cilantro, garlic, and peppercorns in a mortar and pestle to a fine paste. Heat a little more of the reserved oil in a skillet over medium heat, add the paste, and fry until the rawness has gone (you can tell by the look and the smell) and the mixture is fragrant, 1 to 2 minutes. Add the palm sugar and fish sauce and simmer until slightly thickened, about 1 minute. Remove from the heat and add the lime juice, shrimp, and chicken. Stir in half the fried shallots, two-thirds of the fried garlic and two-thirds of the peanuts. Taste for sweet-salt-sour balance and adjust it if you need to, by adding more sugar, fish sauce, or lime juice. Set aside to cool.

Slice the pineapple into quarters, lengthwise. Cut along each length into slices about 1/16 inch thick. Put these on a serving platter; you should have about 30 of them. Spoon 1 teaspoon of the chicken and shrimp mixture on top of each slice, then scatter with the chiles, lime leaves, and cilantro leaves, remaining fried shallots and garlic, and peanuts.

stir-fried shrimp with sugar snaps, basil, chile & lime

A dish I sometimes can't get out of my head until I eat it. It is essential "constant cravings" food. Don't just make it when you're serving this menu; it's a great midweek or Friday night supper, ready in minutes.

serves 6

¾lb raw shelled jumbo shrimp, vein removed

7oz sugar snap peas

1 tablespoon peanut oil

2 red chiles and 1 green chile, halved, seeded, and finely sliced

4 garlic cloves, finely sliced

1 tablespoon fish sauce

2 tablespoons superfine sugar

juice of 1 lime

¾oz basil leaves

sesame seeds, or chopped unsalted peanuts (optional)

Put the shrimp on a double layer of paper towels and dab them with more paper towels to dry: if they're wet they won't fry well.

Halve the sugar snaps along their lengths so you can see the peas peeking out. Heat the peanut oil in a skillet or wok until hot, then add the sugar snaps and stir-fry for about 30 seconds. Add the shrimp, chiles, and garlic, reduce the heat a little, and stir-fry until the shrimp have just turned pink. Throw in the fish sauce, sugar, and lime juice and stir around to help the sugar dissolve, then throw in the basil.

Scatter sesame seeds or chopped peanuts on top, if you like.

korean cucumber salad (*oi muchim*)

This hits my hot-sour-salty-sweet spot. It's good with roast pork, raw fish, even plain rice. Try to get Korean chili powder: it has a round, fruity flavor and isn't too hot.

serves 6

2 cucumbers

2 tablespoons soy sauce

¼ cup rice vinegar

1½ tablespoons each superfine sugar and Korean chili powder, to taste

6 scallions, finely chopped

2 teaspoons sesame oil (optional)

white or black sesame seeds

Cut the cucumber into wafer-thin slices. If you're going to use them immediately, there is no need to salt them.

Mix the soy sauce, vinegar, sugar, and chili powder in a bowl and stir to help the sugar dissolve. Toss the cucumber into the bowl with the scallions and sesame oil, if using, then sprinkle with sesame seeds.

braised pork with ginger & star anise

Dark and glossy, sweet and hot, this is irresistible. You need sweet *kecap manis*—the syrupy and slightly smoky Indonesian soy sauce—but that's not hard to find. If you can't get pork cheeks, use pork shoulder instead (cut it into 1¼-inch cubes) and cook the dish for an hour and a half, rather than three hours.

serves 6

for the pork
2 tablespoons peanut or vegetable oil

3lb 5oz pork cheeks (or see recipe introduction)

2⅔ cups sliced shallots

1¼oz fresh ginger root, peeled and finely grated

8 garlic cloves, finely grated

½ cup *kecap manis*

¼ cup light soy sauce

2 tablespoons tamarind paste

3½ cups chicken stock

1 star anise

3 medium-hot chiles, halved, seeded, and finely chopped

2 bird's-eye chiles, left whole

for the crispy fried shallots
peanut or vegetable oil

1½ cups finely sliced shallots

sea salt flakes

Heat the peanut or vegetable oil in a large, heavy Dutch oven over medium heat. Brown the pork in batches. It doesn't have to get too dark, just golden all over. Remove the pork as you go with a slotted spoon and set aside.

Add the shallots to the pan and cook until they are soft and golden, then add the ginger and garlic. Return the pork to the pan and add the *kecap manis*, soy sauce, tamarind, and stock. Bring to a boil, then immediately reduce the heat to a gentle simmer. Add the star anise and all the chiles and let cook, uncovered, for 3 hours, or until the pork is tender. Take out the star anise (if you can find it) and the whole chiles.

Meanwhile, make the crispy fried shallots. Heat about ¾ inch of peanut or vegetable oil in a sauté pan over medium-high heat. Add the shallots and fry until they're crisp and golden, then scoop them up with a slotted spoon and put them on a double layer of paper towels, to blot off excess oil. Sprinkle with salt.

When the pork is ready, the liquid around it should have reduced down to a gorgeous, glossy, sticky sauce. If you still have too much liquid, lift the pork out with a slotted spoon, set it aside, and reduce the liquid by boiling it. (If you're using pork cheeks, you're unlikely to need to do this.) Cut the pork cheeks into chunks. I don't remove much of their fat—it's part of the flavor—but cut some of it off if you want to. Return the pork to the pan and heat it through.

Serve the pork, either on a warmed platter or in a warmed bowl, with the crispy shallots scattered on top.

jenny's sago *gula melaka*

The great food writer Sri Owen had a party for other food writers before moving house, and among the many desserts offered (some made by Claudia Roden; this wasn't a shabby event) was this. I would never have made it if I'd read the recipe—sago was one of my most loathed school puddings—but sago *gula melaka*, cooked by food writer Jenny Linford, was one of the best things I'd ever tasted. It's refreshing, even though it's sweet, and the texture is nothing like the school puddings of old. The sago sits limpidly in the coconut milk; it's like eating soft pearls. You can find sago and even fresh pandan leaves, also called screwpine leaves, online (see page 252). The latter taste of vanilla but are slightly almondy, too.

serves 6

10½oz fine sago or tapioca pearls

10½oz palm sugar (this is the *gula melaka*), or 1⅓ cups packed soft dark brown sugar

4 pandan leaves

2 x 14oz cans of unsweetened coconut milk

pinch of sea salt flakes

Bring a large saucepan of water to a boil. Add the sago or tapioca pearls and, stirring, return to a boil. Cook for 10 minutes, stirring now and then. Remove from the heat, cover, and let sit for 10 minutes. Uncover the pan, by which time the sago should be translucent, and drain it in a sieve. Rinse the sago under cold running water, drain once more, and set it aside—still in the sieve—for the pearls to drain thoroughly.

Transfer the sago to a serving bowl that you've rinsed with cold water (this just helps the pearls not to stick) and allow it to cool.

Put the palm sugar and 1 cup of water in a heavy saucepan. Tie 2 of the pandan leaves in a knot and add these, too. Bring to a boil, stirring to help the sugar dissolve, then reduce the heat and simmer for 4 minutes until you have a syrup. Scoop out the pandan leaves and put the syrup in a small pitcher. Allow to cool.

Shake the cans of coconut milk, then pour the milk into a saucepan. Tie the remaining 2 pandan leaves in a knot and add to the coconut milk along with the salt. Bring to just under a boil, then reduce the heat to a simmer and cook, stirring, until slightly reduced and thickened. Remove the leaves.

Add some of the coconut milk to the sago, separating the pearls with the back of a wooden spoon and incorporating enough milk to make a loose mixture; this is nothing like as thick as rice pudding, but it shouldn't be too liquid. Serve the extra coconut milk in a small pitcher on the side, with the palm sugar syrup in another. Diners should add as much coconut milk, or syrup, or both, to their pudding as they want.

a perfect lunch

the best of early summer

asparagus, peas & radishes with pistachio pesto

crab, tomato & saffron tart

gooseberry & almond cake with lemon thyme syrup

The title of this menu is a bit cruel, because a perfect lunch is the stuff of dreams. A sprawl of garrulous friends, a rumpled tablecloth, an assortment of glasses and bottles…this scene has been painted, photographed, and filmed. (You can never remember the name of the film, but French "perfect lunch" scenes are invariably presided over by a beautiful woman *d'un certain age*, while the Italian versions feature families with boundless, gesticulating energy.)

In real life, lunches can be more like a scene from a Danish Dogme film (tears, imploding families, bitter truths). Perhaps because I watched too many French and Italian films in my teens and twenties, I've given the perfect lunch a lot of thought and have often strained every sinew in an attempt to deliver it. In the past, I've got up at 6 A.M. to put on slow-cooked pork…and was therefore ready to go back to bed just as everyone arrived. On another occasion a guest took me into the kitchen and started to cry, because her husband was having an affair. I did want to sympathize but, really, I was more worried about overcooking the fish.

Basically I have tried too hard—and not always in the right way—which is why a perfect lunch is a perplexing concept. In our efforts to be generous, to cater for all tastes, and to lavish love, we make dishes that are too complicated, or cook too many of them. (I am totally guilty of this last one, always adding just one more glorious vegetable ensemble.) You, the host and cook, end up back-timing dishes at the stove rather than chatting at the table. The food, because you've evidently put such a lot into it, is praised in a way that stops the flow of conversation (yes, the praise is nice, but it's not the point). By the time the guests leave you're exhausted, and a sense of anticlimax descends as you pack the leftovers into the fridge. It has not been the relaxed affair you envisaged.

But it's difficult, if it isn't part of your birthright—by which I mean you're not French or Italian—to present food just at that perfectly pitched level of casualness. So this is the challenge: to make a lunch that doesn't frazzle you, where the food is good but not spectacular (in that "look what I've made" kind of way), and the number of dishes is limited.

This menu works. The asparagus needs to be cooked at the last minute, but that's do-able. If you don't want to make the pesto, then just serve the asparagus with melted butter, or melted butter and some chunks of creamy, mild goat cheese scattered over the top. The tart crust and filling can be made in advance (keep them separate), then all you have to do is assemble and bake it; it's so rich that complicated side dishes would ruin it, so just compose a green salad. The dessert can be cooked the day before. If you don't want to bake a cake, serve poached gooseberries with whipped cream into which you've stirred some elderflower cordial (shortbread cookies alongside would be good, too).

Although this is a considered meal—it takes advantage of the best ingredients around in early summer—it doesn't require a lot of skill. Enthusiastic cooks will find it hard not to add just one more dish: resist.

asparagus, peas & radishes with pistachio pesto

The pesto here is rich, so you need the radishes to provide a clean contrast.

serves 6

for the pesto

1 cup shelled unsalted pistachios, divided

8 scallions, trimmed and chopped

1 tablespoon unsalted butter

1 fat garlic clove, crushed

¾ cup extra virgin olive oil

4½oz fresh ricotta

½ cup finely grated pecorino or Parmesan cheese

sea salt flakes and freshly ground black pepper

for the vegetables

8 to 10 radishes, preferably French breakfast radishes

1½lb asparagus

3 tablespoons extra virgin olive oil

2½ teaspoons white balsamic vinegar

7oz fresh raw peas

small handful of pea shoots, cress, or microgreens

Start with the pesto. Boil two-thirds of the pistachios in water for 4 minutes; this softens them and makes the pesto creamy. Drain and dry them in a dish cloth. You need to rub off all the papery skin (laborious but therapeutic). Lightly toast the rest of the nuts in a dry skillet for about 30 seconds. You will be able to smell the toasted aroma. Immediately transfer to a plate. Cook the scallions in the butter in a small saucepan until soft, but not colored. Add the garlic and cook for another 30 seconds or so.

Blitz all the nuts with the scallions and garlic in a food processor, gradually adding the extra virgin olive oil. Stir in the ricotta and pecorino or Parmesan. Season and taste.

Now for the vegetables. Shave the radishes using a mandoline slicer, or cut them very finely with a sharp knife.

Break or cut off the base of each asparagus spear (if you use your hands instead of a knife, you can feel where the natural break is). Bring a pan with about 3 inches of water to a boil. Stand the asparagus in this, bases in the water, spears leaning against the side (they cook in the steam). Cover with a lid. Cook until only just tender, testing with a point of a knife. How long it takes depends on the thickness of the asparagus. If it's of average thickness, I reckon on 7 minutes, but I usually start checking after 4.

Lift the asparagus out of the pan, then quickly remove excess moisture by patting it with a clean dish cloth. Add a little of the asparagus cooking water to the pesto to loosen and thin it.

Mix the extra virgin olive oil and the white balsamic vinegar together and season. Divide the asparagus, raw peas, radishes, and pea shoots among 6 plates—or put them all on a platter—and drizzle with the white balsamic dressing. Spoon on some of the pesto and offer the rest at the table.

crab, tomato & saffron tart

This is one of my best dishes and I've been turning it out every summer for years. It's rich, but the custard is delicate. Prepare the components the day before, then you just have to fill the tart crust and bake it.

serves 6 to 8

for the pastry
2 cups all-purpose flour, plus more to dust

1¼ sticks chilled unsalted butter, chopped

good pinch of sea salt flakes

1 medium egg yolk

for the filling
4 plum tomatoes

1 tablespoon unsalted butter

½ tablespoon regular olive oil

1 small onion, very finely chopped

2 garlic cloves, finely chopped

sea salt flakes and freshly ground black pepper

pinch of superfine sugar (optional)

squeeze of lemon juice (optional)

1 scant cup heavy cream

generous pinch of saffron threads

½ cup crème fraîche

1 large egg, plus 3 egg yolks

7oz fresh lump crab meat

1½oz fresh claw crab meat

Put the flour, butter, and salt into a food processor and whiz until the mixture resembles bread crumbs. Mix the yolk with ½ tablespoon of very cold water, add it, and whiz again. The pastry should come together into a ball. Seal in plastic wrap and let rest in the fridge for 20 minutes or so, then roll out on a lightly floured surface and use to line a 9-inch loose-bottomed tart pan. Prick the bottom with a fork, then chill in the fridge or freezer until cold and firm.

Preheat the oven to 350°F and put in a metal baking sheet to heat up. Line the pastry with nonstick parchment paper and fill with pie weights. Place on the hot baking sheet and bake for 14 minutes, removing the paper and weights after 7. Let cool.

Plunge the tomatoes into boiling water and leave them for 20 seconds, then remove. Skin, halve, seed, and cut the flesh into slivers. Heat the butter and regular olive oil in a skillet and cook the onion and tomatoes gently until soft but not colored. Add the garlic, season, and continue to cook until you have a thick purée. Taste. If the tomatoes didn't have the best flavor to begin with, it will benefit from the tiniest bit of sugar and a squeeze of lemon juice. The purée should be dry, not at all wet. Spoon it into the tart crust.

Put about 3 tablespoons of the heavy cream in a saucepan and add the saffron threads. Heat until just under boiling, then stir until you can see the saffron coloring the cream. Let cool. Mix this with the rest of the heavy cream, the crème fraîche, egg, and egg yolks. Season well and gently stir in all the crab. Slowly pour into the tart crust.

Return the tart to the hot baking sheet and cook for 45 minutes, or until the pastry is golden and the filling just set in the middle (it should still have a little give, as it will continue to cook out of the oven). Let cool for 15 minutes, then remove the tart pan and serve.

I think this only needs a green salad, but green snap beans with toasted almonds are also good, and some people always want potatoes…

gooseberry & almond cake with lemon thyme syrup

This is a pale dessert—soft green and cream—which seems just right for early summer. I serve it with extra gooseberries, poached (there's a recipe for them below), but you don't have to.

serves 6 to 8

for the cake

1 stick unsalted butter, softened, plus more for the pan

½ cup superfine sugar, plus ⅓ cup

3 large eggs, at room temperature, lightly beaten

½ cup all-purpose flour, sifted

2 teaspoons chopped lemon thyme leaves

finely grated zest of 1 unwaxed lemon

¾ cup ground almonds (preferably freshly ground)

¾ teaspoon baking powder

¾ lb gooseberries, topped and tailed

for the syrup

¼ cup granulated sugar

juice of 2 large lemons

2 teaspoons lemon thyme leaves

for the poached gooseberries

⅓ cup granulated sugar

2 lemon thyme sprigs

1 lb 2 oz gooseberries, topped and tailed

to serve

thyme flowers, if you can find any

confectioners' sugar, to dust (optional)

sweetened crème fraîche, or whipped cream

Preheat the oven to 375°F. Butter an 8-inch springform cake pan and line the bottom with nonstick parchment paper.

Beat the butter and the ½ cup of superfine sugar until pale and fluffy. Add the eggs a little at a time, beating well after each addition. If the mixture starts to curdle, add 1 tablespoon of the flour. Put the lemon thyme leaves in a mortar and pestle with the lemon zest and pound together to release the fragrance. Add to the batter and briefly mix. Fold in the rest of the flour, the almonds, and the baking powder, using a large metal spoon. Scrape into the pan. Toss the gooseberries with the remaining ⅓ cup of superfine sugar and spread over the top. Bake for 30 minutes.

The cake is ready when a skewer inserted into the center comes out clean. To make the syrup, quickly heat the granulated sugar, lemon juice, and lemon thyme leaves in a saucepan, stirring to help the sugar dissolve. Pierce the cake all over with a skewer while it is still warm and slowly pour the syrup into it. Let cool a little, then carefully remove from the pan and put on a serving plate.

Meanwhile, poach the gooseberries. Heat ¾ cup of water, the granulated sugar, and lemon thyme together in a saucepan, stirring until the sugar has dissolved. Add the gooseberries and cook over medium heat for 4 minutes, or until the fruit is soft but not collapsing (most of the berries should still hold their shape). Let cool.

Any thyme flowers you have will look lovely on top of the cake. You can leave it as it is, or dust lightly with confectioner's sugar just before serving, with sweetened crème fraîche or whipped cream and the poached gooseberries on the side.

before the *passeggiata*

a southern italian supper

fennel *taralli*

burrata with fennel, roast bell peppers, anchovies & capers

spaghetti & shellfish *al cartoccio*

ricotta, candied lemon peel & pistachio ice cream

Southern Italy is the Italy of the northern European imagination. I grew up, in a Northern Irish seaside town, visiting an ice cream parlor—Morelli's—that had a picture of the Amalfi coast running along one wall. I was mesmorized, at six years old, that such a place could exist. The sea was cobalt blue, the flowers scarlet. It was so unlike the choppy, pewter Atlantic the café looked out over. When I eventually got to the south of Italy, as an adult, it was all I had hoped for and more. Amalfi, Sorrento, and Ravello, with their terraces of citrus trees and floods of bougainvillea, all linked by a cliff-hugging ribbon of road, are patchworks of color, light, and stone. At least, they are in the warmer months. My first trip there was to a wintry Amalfi. The lemon trees were wrapped in gray gauze to protect them from hailstones—making them look like ghosts—and the sea was dark and angry.

Over the years, the southern Italy I have come to love more is far from the carefree, monied ease of Ravello; it is more chaotic, muscular, vigorous, and poorer. Naples, where the air smells of coffee, fried dough, and the sea; Sicily, where they eat ice cream and brioche for breakfast; Polignano a Mare in Puglia, where the *passeggiata* feels like a festival (the *passeggiata*, an evening promenade, is about showing off and letting go of the day, giving a damn and yet not giving a damn).

Your first hour in Naples makes you wonder what drug you've been slipped. It's both frightening and exhilarating. You feel it might implode and you have no idea, at first, how to find its center, and I don't mean its physical center, but its emotional one. The city seems unmappable, unknowable. There's noise—shouting, car horns, the throaty gurgle of the Vespas that perilously take every street corner—and activity (gossiping, drinking, smoking) everywhere. Small streets crisscross and veer off at odd angles, slivers of sea float into view when you least expect them, then disappear, cars are parked almost on top of each other, vendors (often elderly ladies wrapped in shawls) sell motley collections of goods: lighters, plastic toys, and mysterious liqueurs. There are layers—of hanging laundry, of crumbling plaster, of paint and posters and history—and colors appear saturated. It can be hard to work out where to focus.

Strategic and beautiful, Naples has been fought over and colonized by Greeks, Romans, Normans, and Spanish. It has seen it all and survived and its fighting spirit is evident. It's not a place for ritzy restaurants; you eat on the hoof, grabbing a slice of pizza then, later, a *sflogliatella* (a shell-shaped layered pastry stuffed with ricotta and orange peel) or some ice cream. There has been complex, aristocratic cooking here. Queen Maria Caroline de Bourbon, Marie-Antoinette's sister, brought French chefs to her court in the 18th century, to inject some sophistication. These chefs, known as *monzus* (a corruption of monsieur) fused down-to-earth Neapolitan food, such as macaroni, with French complexity. Today it's hard to see that influence, though you find babas in pastry shops and crème patissière (*crema pasticcera*) is used.

Now the cooking of Naples, and all of southern Italy, is direct, intense, and imaginative, the product of the genius of home cooks, who need to make the best of vegetables, pasta, pulses, bread, and leftovers. They know how to turn bread crumbs into something so delicious (frying them until golden, crunchy, and perfumed with olive oil and garlic) that you eat them on pasta and don't miss Parmesan.

Then there's leftover risotto, formed into cones or balls, stuffed with cheese or ragù, and deep-fried until they are simultaneously soothing and explosive. Limitations can be a powerfully creative force; they encourage care. If you only have tomatoes, garlic, onions, and olive oil you will work out how to make the best tomato sauce, even slightly different versions according to your mood or the time of year. That's partly why you can eat pasta with tomato sauce in southern Italy and marvel at its depth.

Sometimes it seems wrong to rhapsodize what is essentially a *cucina povera*. We forget the actual poor. This hit me when I got lost in Palermo years ago. In a cramped residential area I stumbled across an old woman, sitting in a small garage: her home. There was an old wrought-iron bed with a stained mattress, bags of clothes, a gas stove with a coffee pot. She sat in a plastic deck chair and around her, on the ground, was the peel of a dozen or more oranges. She was still greedily eating them and offered one to me. Sicilian oranges are some of the best in the world, but they're probably not so great if they're the only thing you have to eat.

As well as care, ordinary ingredients need strong flavors to make them seductive, the flavors of peperoncini, (*la droga dei poveri*, "the drug of the poor"), garlic, oregano, cured anchovies, capers… But you can also find the mild and the gentle here. In Puglia, burrata (which means "buttery") oozes cream and smells of new milk. Slice tomatoes or ripe peaches and eat them with this, black pepper, salt, and extra virgin olive oil. Why would you cook? In Sicily you can buy ricotta that's still warm, the curds just holding together, sitting in its basket like a newborn milky wonder (it's hard not to scoop it up on your fingers and eat it as you cook). The last time I was there I cooked green beans, tossed them with oil, lemon juice, and chile, and put little nuggets of ricotta on top. It was the best thing I ate.

As well as the simplicity of southern Italian food, I love the Arab legacy. Not only did they bring ingredients—citrus trees and sugar and eggplants—but they brought their blending of savory with sweet, which you see so clearly in the food of Sicily. There's also a mad passion for the sweet and the decorative (though food historians can't agree whether this is from the Arabs or not), including fruits and animals made from marzipan. They're most in evidence in Sicily. One Easter I watched Corrado Costanzo, owner of one of the island's most famous *gelatiere*, sculpt these with his large hands. With turns and flicks of his wrist, lumps of marzipan were transformed—he used only a few small tools, then applied color with tiny brushes—into doll-sized lemons and blushing apricots. They appeared so fluidly I was sure he must be performing some sleight of hand.

They have a saying in Naples, "It doesn't matter whether we're governed by France or Spain so long as we eat," and you get that sense all over southern Italy. There's a hedonism—it may have developed out of a simple need for self-preservation—that seems like a good attitude to me.

Negronis aren't a southern Italian drink—Campari and other bitter drinks were created in the back rooms of bars in northern Italy—but it's my favorite way to kick off any Italian meal. Pour yourself one before anyone arrives. Hedonism, remember…

fennel *taralli*

Taralli—little bread rings with a "knot" on one side—are common in southern Italy. They're straightforward (though time-consuming) to make and good with drinks. Italian delis often sell them, if you don't want to make your own. I sometimes add crushed red pepper to the dough as well as fennel seeds.

makes about 60

½ cup lukewarm dry
white wine

scant ½ cup lukewarm water

1 teaspoon superfine sugar

2 teaspoons active dry yeast

4 cups all-purpose flour, plus
more to dust

sea salt flakes and freshly ground
black pepper

1 tablespoon fennel seeds,
roughly bashed in a mortar

scant ½ cup extra virgin olive oil,
plus more to handle the dough

Mix the wine, water, and sugar, add the yeast, and stir it all together. Let stand somewhere warm until the mixture becomes frothy. This might take a little longer than usual, up to 25 minutes.

Put the flour in a bowl with the salt, pepper, and fennel seeds and make a well in the middle. Add the extra virgin olive oil to the yeast liquid and pour this gradually into the dry ingredients, mixing as you do so. Bring into a ball and knead by hand for 10 minutes, or in a mixer fitted with a dough hook. The dough should become smooth and elastic.

Clean and lightly oil the bowl and put the dough into it, coating it lightly with oil by turning it over. Cover the top of the bowl with plastic wrap and let stand in a warm spot to rise for 1 to 1¼ hours. The dough should be puffed up but not quite doubled in size.

Line 2 baking sheets with nonstick parchment paper and lightly oil or flour the paper (this makes it easier to move the *taralli*). Take little handfuls of the dough and roll each into a rope about 18 inches long and ½ inch in diameter. Cut each rope into 3 equal pieces and join the ends—twisting into a knot—to form a ring. Place on the prepared baking sheets. Cover loosely with plastic wrap and let stand to prove for 1 hour.

Preheat the oven to 350°F. Bring a large pot of water to a boil. Carefully remove 4 to 5 *taralli* from the baking sheets and drop them into the boiling water. As soon as they float to the surface, remove them with a slotted spoon and return them to the baking sheets. When they are all blanched, bake on the middle rack of the oven for 30 minutes.

Take the baking sheets out of the oven, turn the rings over and reduce the oven temperature to 225°F. Bake for another 30 minutes, or until completely hard, dry, and crisp. Let cool, then store in airtight containers for up to 1 week.

burrata with fennel, roast bell peppers, anchovies & capers

It took a long time for burrata—a rich cream-stuffed mozzarella—to get to Great Britain and the United States, but thank goodness it arrived. It oozes lactic sweetness. It's also the perfect focal point for a dish that requires few other ingredients: start with good burrata and there isn't much that can go wrong. Here, the saltiness of anchovies and capers and the sweetness of bell peppers are excellent counterpoints. The fennel isn't just for its aniseed flavor, but also for crunch.

serves 4

4 red bell peppers, halved and seeded

regular olive oil

sea salt flakes and freshly ground black pepper

1 medium fennel bulb

about ¼ cup lemon juice, divided

2 tablespoons coarsely chopped flat-leaf parsley leaves

small handful of basil leaves, coarsely torn

about 12 mint leaves, torn

⅓ cup extra virgin olive oil, plus more to serve

10oz burrata

12 anchovies in olive oil (use a good-quality brand, such as Ortiz), chopped

2 tablespoons capers, rinsed and patted dry

Preheat the oven to 375°F.

Place the bell pepper halves in a roasting pan, drizzle with regular olive oil, and season. Roast for 30 minutes, or until soft and slightly scorched in places. Let cool, then cut into strips. (You can peel the skin off of the bell peppers if you like, but I rarely bother.)

Trim the tips of the fennel, then halve the bulb lengthwise. Cut the core out of each piece and remove any tough or discolored outer leaves. Put about 3 tablespoons of the lemon juice in a bowl. Either shave each piece of fennel on a mandoline slicer, or slice it very finely with a sharp knife. You want to end up with wafer-thin slices. Toss in the lemon juice to stop it from discoloring.

Mix the herbs together with the extra virgin olive oil, ½ tablespoon of the lemon juice, and some seasoning. Taste and adjust the seasoning, adding more lemon juice if you want. Lift the burrata out of its liquid and carefully set it on paper towels to drain a little, otherwise the milky liquid seeps into the olive oil.

Put the burrata on a serving plate with the bell pepper and fennel alongside. Scatter with the chopped anchovies and the capers, then spoon on the herb dressing. Lightly dress the burrata with more extra virgin olive oil and serve immediately.

spaghetti & shellfish *al cartoccio*

This might seem a hassle, but the paper parcels aren't just for show. The pasta, which cooks with the seafood, becomes wonderfully flavored with the fish. The aroma as you open the parcels is great, too: pure Mediterranean seaside. It's really worth doing (though hard to pull off for more than four diners).

serves 4

2¼lb mussels

2½ tablespoons extra virgin olive oil, plus more for the parcels and pasta

1 small onion, very finely chopped

3 garlic cloves, finely sliced

¼ teaspoon crushed red pepper

6 large tomatoes, peeled, seeded, and chopped (see page 35)

scant 1 cup dry white vermouth

2 tablespoons finely chopped flat-leaf parsley leaves

1lb spaghetti

1½lb raw shelled jumbo shrimp, veined removed

sea salt flakes and freshly ground black pepper

Preheat the oven to 350°F. Clean the mussels, removing beards and barnacles (scrape the latter off with a knife) and washing shells. Tap each against the sink and discard any that are open and don't close.

Heat 2 tablespoons of the extra virgin olive oil in a pan large enough to hold the mussels. Add the onion and cook until soft but not colored. Add the garlic, crushed red pepper, and tomatoes, increase the heat a little and cook for another 3 minutes. Add the vermouth and bring to a boil. Reduce the heat to medium, add the mussels, and cook for 2 minutes, or until they open, shaking the pan a couple of times and throwing in the parsley for the last 30 seconds or so. When the mussels are cooked, remove and discard any that haven't opened. Take half the mussels out, remove the meat from the shells, return the meat to the pan, and cover to keep warm.

Put together 4 double rectangles of parchment paper (for extra strength), each about 17½ x 10½ inches. Brush the center of each with a little extra virgin olive oil. Lightly oil 2 roasting pans, too.

Parboil the pasta in lots of boiling lightly salted water for 7 minutes. Drain and moisten it with extra virgin olive oil. Heat the remaining ½ tablespoon of extra virgin olive oil in a skillet and quickly sauté the shrimp, just long enough to get a very pale pink color: they will continue to cook in the parcels. Season.

Divide the pasta between the parcels, putting it in the middle. Add the shrimp and mussels with their sauce. (Don't add so much sauce that it starts to run across the paper; it should cling to the pasta and seafood.) Season, then drizzle each portion with a little extra virgin olive oil. Carefully pull the 2 longer edges of each parcel together, turning them over to seal (don't roll it up so the parcel is tight, you want to make a kind of tent). Now seal each parcel by turning over the ends as well. Carefully move them to the roasting pans and bake for 7 minutes. Transfer the parcels to plates—again, be careful—and serve.

ricotta, candied lemon peel & pistachio ice cream

This is an incredibly easy ice cream to make, as it doesn't require a custard base. It sets hard, so you need to take it out of the freezer thirty minutes before you want to serve it (or longer if your kitchen is quite cool). It's blissfully springlike. This makes more than you need, but it's harder to churn in small quantities.

makes about 1 quart

1lb 2oz fresh ricotta

3 tablespoons whole milk

scant 1 cup heavy cream

¾ cup superfine sugar

finely grated zest of 1 unwaxed lemon, plus juice of 1½ lemons

⅓ cup candied lemon peel, plus more to serve (optional)

¼ cup coarsely chopped shelled unsalted pistachios, plus more to serve (optional)

Mash the ricotta in a bowl and gradually add the milk and cream, whisking with a fork or a balloon whisk so that everything mixes well together. Add the sugar and zest, stirring to help the sugar dissolve. Cover and put in the fridge to chill.

Add the lemon juice and churn in an ice-cream machine, or transfer to a shallow container and put in the freezer. If you're using the latter manual method, take the ice cream out and churn it—either using an electric hand mixer or by putting the mixture in a food processor—3 times during the freezing process. Do this first after about 1 hour, when the mixture is setting around the edges, then at 2-hour intervals. Cover with a lid, or with plastic wrap or parchment paper, between each churning, and also when you store it.

When the ice cream is still a little soft, mix in the candied lemon peel and pistachios. Freeze until needed, then serve sprinkled with more candied lemon peel and pistachios, if you like.

if you're going to san francisco

cooking for alice and joyce and judy

elderflower gin & tonic

spinach & ricotta *gnudi*

leg of lamb stuffed with lemon & many herbs

sarassou | fava beans with lettuce, shallots & mint

pink grapefruit & basil ice cream

On a rainy afternoon in 1985, I walked into a bookshop in north London and found a volume that has moved between my bedside table, desk, and kitchen ever since. It was the *Chez Panisse Menu Cookbook*, by Alice Waters. I knew who Waters was—I'd read a piece about her and her restaurant in Berkeley— but I didn't know much about her cooking style. British food lovers, at that time, were in thrall to nouvelle cuisine. We were buying hexagonal plates and reducing quarts of veal stock (I regularly carried 30 pounds of veal bones home on the subway). Chefs pushed tiny diamonds of red bell pepper into position with tweezers. The dishes were complex and the menu descriptions ("pillows of fish mousse nestling in a nage") ludicrous.

I stood and leafed through the Chez Panisse menus—baked garlic with goat cheese, charcoal-grilled pork with roasted bell peppers, plum sherbet—and my spine tingled. I felt as if I'd plunged into the sea, such was the freshness of this food. I could immediately taste it and see it. It was bold because it was simple, and it had a kind of magic. For Alice, a bowl of fresh cherries with home-made almond cookies was a good dessert. I immediately understood this woman. Furthermore, Alice, like me, loved menus.

Chez Panisse served a set dinner every day. This gave the cooking a definite style, a clarity. Alice understood the importance of a well-dressed salad, too, the dish I learned to value more than any other during my own time in France.

People have often said that Alice cooked Californian produce with a Mediterranean sensibility. In fact, her approach was shaped by living in Paris. It wasn't the sun that was important, but the care with which food was cooked, the importance placed on ingredients, the way producers (farmers, growers, bakers) were valued. I'd already taken this message from home—it was something I grew up with—but as you cook it's easy to lose your way. For years when I felt this was happening, when I was trying to do tricksy things (like getting two sauces to meet in a line on the plate), or was being seduced by some fad, I went back to the *Chez Panisse Menu Cookbook*. I only needed to read a few of the menus and I'd be back on track. It was my lodestar.

I visited Chez Panisse for the first time in 1992. It was the highlight of a meticulously planned American food trip: three weeks, eating in restaurants I'd been dreaming about for years. I sat across the road in the car for half an hour just looking at it before I went in.

Inside it was all candles and glowing wood. The meal—salt cod gratin, grilled lamb with black olives, Marsala-baked pears—was everything I had hoped for: great ingredients, nothing extraneous. I still have the menu. I ate in other places that week, and discovered how many chefs had passed through the Chez Panisse kitchen, taking its philosophy with them. I ate the late Judy Rodger's roast chicken at Zuni Café and a Mediterranean feast from Joyce Goldstein at Square One. I bought so many books by Californian chefs that I had to purchase an extra suitcase for them. What I saw and ate in that short period—again and again—was an honesty, a kind of plain and simple beauty. Cooks here cared about a perfect goat cheese and a good roast chicken, in the same way as the French did, but their food had more energy. There was also more diversity in California—Asian and Mexican food as well as Mediterranean—and the ingredients, the lemons and figs and melons, seemed more intense, saturated with color.

Back in London I held on to my San Francisco connection via books. I cooked from them, of course, and while in Books for Cooks, the tiny bookshop I visited often, I was always to be found in the American section.

When I eventually gave up my job as a television producer and started to write, I sent my first book, *Crazy Water, Pickled Lemons*, to Joyce Goldstein, the most Mediterranean- and North Africa-loving of the three San Francisco chefs I most admired. I didn't expect to hear from her, but she loved the book and wrote to me. This started a correspondence that has gone on ever since. Over the years she has sent me her books and I've sent her mine. We met—finally—when I was in the States on a publicity tour. She held a dinner for me in San Francisco; I had to go and have a cry halfway through.

I finally realized only last year, while deep in conversation with Alice about her memoir, what had really got to me thirty years before about the whole Northern Californian Chez Panisse philosophy. It was the care they all took—over the typeface used for the menus, the candles, the flowers, the dishes, the produce—it was about valuing the ordinary, seeing the beauty in the small things. It was about caring that you can buy good cherries—that everyone can—and knowing that serving these cherries to friends is a good thing, just because they're beautiful and they taste good.

Alice kept using the word "love," not just about people, but about all sorts of things: early evening light, candles, mulberry ice cream, hats, peaches. She is a sensualist, as are all the Californian chefs I admire.

They notice everything that you can see and taste and smell. And their lives are richer for it. I think this is what I immediately picked up on in that book shop. The *Chez Panisse Menu Cookbook* is not just a cookbook, it is a way of seeing things, which is why I keep going back to it.

I know it seems strange—this Northern Irish woman cleaving to a West Coast approach to food and to life—but when Joyce Goldstein gave that dinner, I felt I was absolutely in the right place. And when she stood up and said that my books made me an honorary Californian, a San Franciscan cook, it was the highest compliment she could have paid me.

elderflower gin & tonic

This drink is local and seasonal to me, in Great Britain, in early summer, so it seems a perfect way to start a meal that honors this philosophy.

makes 2 generous cups

for the elderflower gin
20 just-picked elderflower heads

18fl oz gin

⅓ cup superfine sugar

to serve
tonic water, lime slices, and mint sprigs

Shake the elderflowers gently to dislodge any little bugs that might be hiding in them. Pour the gin into a big preserving jar and add the flowers and the sugar. Close the jar and shake it every day for 1 week.

Strain the mixture through a sieve lined with some cheesecloth, then pour into a clean bottle.

Put 1½oz elderflower gin in a glass with ice. Top off with tonic and add lime slices and mint sprigs.

spinach & ricotta *gnudi*

Tender little dumplings, as fragile as a pasta filling, which is how they got their name: *gnudi* is Tuscan dialect for "naked" (and Michelangelo's paintings of nude figures in the Sistine Chapel were referred to as *ignudi*). I adore these. They take a bit of time to make, but I love the process; you need a light touch, as forming them is like handling flowers. I am sometimes tempted to complicate *gnudi*—adding strips of prosciutto, lightly cooked fava beans or peas (and all of these are fine additions)—but they're best naked, served with nothing more than melted butter.

serves 6

9oz fresh ricotta

1lb spinach, coarse stalks removed

2 tablespoons unsalted butter, plus 3½ tablespoons to serve

¼ small onion, very finely chopped

2 medium egg yolks

1 cup finely grated Parmesan cheese, plus more to serve

freshly grated nutmeg

¼ cup all-purpose flour, plus more to dust

sea salt flakes and freshly ground black pepper

Put the ricotta in a sieve lined with cheesecloth. Let stand for a couple of hours to allow the excess moisture to drain off.

Wash the spinach and put it in a large pan with the water that's left clinging to the leaves. Cover and set over medium heat to wilt for 5 to 6 minutes, turning the leaves over halfway through. Pour into a colander and let cool, then squeeze out every bit of moisture either with your fists or by putting the spinach—in batches—between 2 dinner plates and pressing them together. Chop the spinach finely.

Melt the 2 tablespoons of butter and gently sauté the onion until soft but not colored. Add the spinach and stir it around; more moisture should evaporate in the heat of the pan. Scrape the spinach into a bowl and let cool, then mix in the ricotta, egg yolks, Parmesan, nutmeg, flour, and seasoning. Taste a little of the raw mixture for seasoning.

Sprinkle a dusting of flour onto a large baking pan. Using wet hands (these work better than floured hands), roll the mixture into nuggets, a bit smaller than a walnut, then roll each gently in the flour to coat lightly. Put on a plate, cover with plastic wrap, and refrigerate for 1 hour, or up to 1 day, to firm them up (the chilling here is vital).

Bring a really big saucepan of lightly salted water to a boil, then reduce the heat to a simmer. Melt the 3½ tablespoons of butter in a large skillet or sauté pan, then take it off the heat. Cook the *gnudi* in batches by dropping them into the water. After a couple of minutes they should have bobbed to the surface, so lift them out with a slotted spoon and drop them into the butter. Shake them around a little and cover the pan. When all the *gnudi* are cooked, gently heat them through in the butter.

Serve in warmed dishes, sprinkling with a little more Parmesan and grinding on some black pepper.

leg of lamb stuffed with lemon & many herbs

This lamb came about because I couldn't decide which herb to choose, so I just used several together, and I've now been making it for thirty years. The herb paste permeates every bit of the meat. Because it's simple, I usually serve it with an unusual—but not complicated—side dish. The *sarassou* recipe on page 56 is excellent with the lamb, radishes, and potatoes.

serves 6

for the lamb
3 tablespooons flat-leaf parsley leaves, coarsely chopped

leaves from 10 thyme sprigs

needles from 2 rosemary sprigs, chopped

4 garlic cloves, chopped, plus another 6

sea salt flakes and freshly ground black pepper

⅓ cup extra virgin olive oil

finely grated zest of 1 unwaxed lemon

4lb leg of lamb

for the vegetables
big bunch of French breakfast radishes with good fresh, perky leaves

1lb 9oz baby waxy potatoes

The day before you want to serve the lamb, put the herbs, 4 chopped garlic cloves, salt, and pepper into a mortar and grind to a paste, gradually working in the extra virgin olive oil and lemon zest as you do so. Make incisions all over the lamb with a sharp knife and loosen the meat around the protruding bone (at the tapered end of the joint) to about one-third of the way into the leg.

Rub the paste all over the lamb, down inside it, around the bone, and into the incisions. Cut the remaining 6 garlic cloves into slivers, then push these down into the incisions as well. Cover loosely with plastic wrap or foil and refrigerate for 24 hours, bringing it to room temperature before roasting (it will take about 2 hours for it to come to room temperature).

Preheat the oven to 425°F.

Put the lamb in a roasting pan and cook it for 15 minutes, then reduce the oven temperature to 350°F and roast for another 45 minutes. The lamb will be pink. If you prefer it more well done, then cook for a little longer.

Cover with foil, insulate well (I use old towels or dish cloths for this), and let rest for 15 minutes. Transfer to a warmed serving plate. Quickly heat the juices in the roasting pan and serve them in a small sauceboat alongside; there may not be much, but that's okay, it's not supposed to be a "gravy."

Meanwhile, carefully wash the radishes (trying not to squash the leaves). Gently dry them and put on a serving platter. Boil the potatoes until they are tender, drain, season with salt, and add to the platter with the radishes. Serve with the lamb and the *sarassou* and fava beans on page 56.

sarassou

I'm very fond of the various cheese-based dishes (sometimes there's little difference between them) that the French serve with vegetables, bread, or crudités (*claqueret, cervelle de canut, fromage fort*). *Sarassou* (also known as *sarasson*) used to be made with buttermilk, but is now usually made with fromage frais (also known as fromage blanc) from either cow or goat milk. (I sometimes add a little soft goat cheese to it, for more tang.) In some parts of France, it's served with bread, in others potatoes, and also with pork and lentils. It's very good—if unusual—within this menu of hot lamb and cold peppery radishes. I prefer it made with a mixture of fromage frais and crème fraîche, but make it with fromage frais alone, if you prefer. Don't use low-fat stuff, though.

serves 6

½ cup fromage frais

½ cup crème fraîche

1 teaspoon white wine vinegar

½ garlic clove, finely grated

finely grated zest of ¼ unwaxed lemon

3½ tablespoons finely snipped chives

sea salt flakes and freshly ground black pepper

To make the *sarassou*, just stir everything together, taste, then adjust the seasoning. Cover and keep in the fridge (but take it out about 1 hour before you want to serve it; it shouldn't be served fridge-cold).

Serve with the lamb, potatoes, radishes, and fava beans.

fava beans with lettuce, shallots & mint

serves 6

1lb 9oz fava beans in the pod (this will yield about 2¼ cups fresh beans)

3½ tablespoons unsalted butter

6 shallots, finely chopped

1 small head romaine lettuce

sea salt flakes and freshly ground black pepper

good squeeze of lemon juice

leaves from 6 mint sprigs, torn

Cook the fava beans in boiling water for 4 minutes, then drain and run cold water over them. Once they are cool enough to handle, slip off their skins. This is laborious, but the color is quite brilliant, and you can prepare them earlier in the day up to this point.

Melt the butter in a large skillet and sauté the shallots over medium-low heat until soft but not colored. Cut the base off the lettuce and shred the leaves. Add them to the shallots and cook over medium heat until wilted, then add the beans. Heat through, season, then add the lemon juice and mint. Serve in a broad, warmed bowl.

pink grapefruit & basil ice cream

This is possibly the best ice cream I've ever made. I'd been doing a good lemon and basil ice cream for years…then it struck me that the bitterness of grapefruit might work well with the almost cloying sweetness of basil. I was right. The color will vary depending on the juice of your grapefruit, sometimes it is very pale pink, sometimes almost coral-colored. Remove the ice cream from the freezer about 10 minutes before you want to serve it, to allow it to soften a little.

serves 6

finely grated zest and juice of
1 pink grapefruit

¼ cup granulated sugar

1¼ cups whole milk

35 basil leaves

4 large egg yolks

⅓ cup superfine sugar

⅔ cup heavy cream

1 to 2 tablespoons lemon juice

Put the grapefruit zest and granulated sugar into a mortar and pound with the pestle. Heat the milk with the pounded zest mixture until it reaches boiling point. Remove from the heat and coarsely tear and add the basil leaves. Cover and set aside to infuse for a couple of hours.

Using an electric hand mixer, beat the egg yolks with the superfine sugar until pale and thick. Strain the flavored milk into a glass measuring cup, using the back of a spoon to press out all the flavor from the basil and the grapefruit zest. Stir this into the egg mixture and put it into a clean, heavy pan. Over low heat, stirring all the time, heat the custard until it thickens slightly. It needs to be thick enough to coat the back of a spoon (you should be able to run your finger through it and leave a channel). Be really careful, as the eggs will scramble if it gets too hot. Immediately pour it into a cool bowl (I set the bowl in a sink full of water and ice cubes, to help stop the cooking immediately). Let the custard stand until it reaches room temperature, stirring from time to time as it cools.

Whip the cream to soft peaks, being careful not to overbeat it. Fold into the custard, then stir in the grapefruit juice and 1 tablespoon of the lemon juice. Taste before adding any more lemon juice: it should enhance the grapefruit flavor, not overwhelm it.

Churn in an ice-cream machine, or transfer to a shallow container and put in the freezer. If you're using the manual method, take the ice cream out and churn it—either using an electric hand mixer or by putting the mixture in a food processor—3 times during the freezing process. Do this first after about 1 hour, when the mixture is setting around the edges, then at 2-hour intervals. Cover with a lid, or with plastic wrap, between each churning, and when you store it.

Serve with plain cookies, or on its own. It doesn't need anything else.

my spanish cupboard

anchovies, artichokes, and fideuà

pan con tomate with anchovies

vegetable *fideuà* with saffron & allioli

zurra jellies with strawberries in sherry

Because food is, for me, so much about place, I try to keep ingredients from particular countries together. Most are in my biggest kitchen cupboard, the different groups sitting alongside each other, but a few countries get their own small cupboard. Arranging ingredients this way makes it easier to find things— you can't have your pomegranate molasses hidden by bottles of Thai fish sauce—but really I do it because it means I can think about where I want to go, through cooking.

Having grown up in Northern Ireland—where it was hard to find unusual ingredients—I was overwhelmed when I moved to London, where you could buy almost anything. There was no internet then, so all the foods I needed for dishes from Spain or Vietnam or the Middle East had to be tracked down. I would set off with a list of addresses, an *A-Z of London*, and a travel card for the subway. When I got home I would unwrap packages, sniff the ingredients (dried shrimp paste is the only one that ever made me recoil; still does), and put everything carefully in groups.

An additional pleasure in organizing foods this way is being able to look at the packaging, and Spain— which has its own cupboard—has the most colorful and timeless. There are scarlet-and-yellow cans of Ortiz tuna and anchovies (their design hasn't changed for decades); fat cloth sacks of paella rice; cans of olive oil, from the regal looking Núñez de Prado to the childlike can of L'Estornell with its illustration of a little bird; packets of *turrón* tied up with ribbon; tiny jars of saffron and various cans of smoked paprika, in tones of rust and azure blue. These make my heart sing. I've cooked with these ingredients for so many years that they're now familiar—using them is comforting—and yet they still also bring a frisson, the excitement of the unknown. I can visit Spain in dishes old and new, and my own past, simply through tins and packets and the smells in my kitchen. It's a cupboard of possibilities.

pan con tomate with anchovies

Pan con tomate is a Catalan dish (there it's known as *pa amb tomàquet*), though it's equally loved all over Spain, especially in Majorca; you can read about it in Tomás Graves's lovely book on the island, *Bread and Oil*. It's just bread, usually toasted, sometimes rubbed with garlic, sometimes not, with extra virgin olive oil and crushed tomatoes. What's interesting is that *pan con tomate* has the same ingredients as Italian bruschetta with tomatoes, but it's so different. I can have *bruschetta al pomodoro* and not end up messy, but *pan con tomate* leaves me wiping oil off my face. Eating it is visceral in a way that feels very Spanish to me. It's about greed, hunger, oil-smeared skin. Some people make it by simply crushing a halved tomato on the bread until you are left with just the skin (you see? That's what you do when you have pure tomato lust) but it works better if you grate the tomato flesh. Grating gives you tomato "water" along with the pulp. When you're getting to the end of the tomato pulp, you can extend it by adding some of the tomato water. You can obviously serve this without anchovies if you're cooking for vegetarians but, you know, salt…(irresistible).

serves 6

4 really well-flavored plum tomatoes

extra virgin olive oil, preferably Spanish

sea salt flakes and freshly ground black pepper

½ flat, rustic loaf, such as a flat sourdough or ciabatta

2 garlic cloves, halved horizontally

12 good-quality anchovies in oil, such as Ortiz

Cut the tomatoes in half. Rub the flat side of each half against the coarse-holed side of a box grater that you have placed in a bowl. Once all the flesh has been grated, discard the skins. Transfer the grated tomato pulp to a nylon mesh strainer set over a separate bowl, then let stand for 30 minutes.

Put the drained pulp in a bowl, reserving the tomato "water" that dripped through the sieve, stir 2 teaspoons of extra virgin olive oil into the pulp, and season.

Cut the loaf into 6 pieces, each about 3¼ inches wide, then horizontally halve each piece so you have the fluffy insides exposed. Grill or toast the pieces of bread. Rub the halved garlic on the surface of the once-fluffy, now-charred sides.

Spoon some of the reserved tomato water on top and let it soak in (you won't use all of it). Spoon some of the tomato-oil mixture onto each piece of toast, too, crushing it more as you do so with the back of a spoon. The idea is to infuse the bread with the tomatoes, not make a pizza. Sprinkle with a little more extra virgin olive oil and put a couple of anchovies on each piece.

vegetable *fideuà* with saffron & allioli

Fideuà—which is made exactly like a paella, but with thin noodles instead of rice—is a genius dish. The pasta is added to boiling stock, which it absorbs (and which reduces) as the dish cooks. *Fideuà* made with fish is also excellent, and very rich. You can buy the correct noodles in Spanish grocery stores and online (see page 252 for sources).

serves 6

for the allioli
2 large garlic cloves
sea salt flakes and freshly ground white pepper
2 large egg yolks
¼ teaspoon Dijon mustard
1¼ cups extra virgin olive oil (fruity or buttery, not grassy)
lemon juice, to taste
white wine vinegar, to taste

for the fideuà
1 small or ½ medium fennel bulb
1lb 10oz fava beans (in the pod), to yield 2¼ cups fresh beans
3 tablespoons extra virgin olive oil, divided
1 onion, finely chopped
1 red bell pepper, seeded, chopped
¾lb plum tomatoes, coarsely chopped
3 teaspoons smoked paprika
4 cups chicken or vegetable stock
really generous pinch of saffron threads
freshly ground black pepper
12oz *fideos* noodles
8 artichoke hearts in olive oil, from a jar, thickly sliced

For the allioli, crush the garlic to a paste with a little salt in a mortar, then transfer it to a bowl. Using a wooden spoon, mix in the egg yolks and mustard and stir until glossy. Beating, either with the wooden spoon or an hand mixer, start adding the extra virgin olive oil in tiny drops. Only add more oil when the previous drop has been well incorporated and the mixture has thickened. You can add larger amounts of oil as it thickens. If the allioli splits, just start again with a new egg yolk, and gradually add the curdled mixture to it.

Season with the white pepper and add the lemon juice and vinegar little by little, tasting until you're happy. I know I haven't given quantities for vinegar or lemon juice, but that would be pointless, as you need to use your taste buds. Vinegars vary in acidity, while the quantity of lemon juice or vinegar you need is also affected by the amount of salt you add. Start by adding 1 teaspoon each of lemon juice and vinegar, then keep tasting. Cover the allioli and put it in the fridge until you need it.

Trim the tops from the fennel, reserving any feathery fronds. Halve the bulb lengthwise and remove the coarse outer layer of leaves. Trim off and discard the base and chop the rest of the flesh.

Remove the beans from the pods and cook in boiling water for about 4 minutes. Drain in a colander and run cold water over them. Let cool, then slip the skin off each bean (it's worth it for the emerald green color).

Heat 2 tablespoons of the extra virgin olive oil in a broad, shallow pan about 12 inches across. Cook the onion over medium heat until soft and pale gold, then add the bell pepper and tomatoes and cook, stirring, until soft and thick (reduce the heat if anything starts to brown). Add the fennel and fronds and cook for 5 minutes, then add the paprika. Cook for 2 minutes, then add the stock and saffron. Bring to a boil, stirring so the saffron infuses the stock. Season well.

Add the noodles, reduce the heat to a gentle simmer, and let cook for about 12 minutes. During this time the pasta will absorb the stock and become soft. It's important not to stir.

About 4 minutes before the end of cooking time, add the artichoke hearts to the *fideuà*, then, in the last couple of minutes, quickly sauté the cooked fava beans in the remaining 1 tablespoon of extra virgin olive oil. Season. Add the fava beans to the *fideuà*; they need to be well distributed, but try not to stir the pasta too much because it releases starch and makes the dish sticky.

Serve with the allioli on the side. You don't need anything else.

zurra jellies with strawberries in sherry

Zurra is white sangria, made with cava, and these jellies are based on that drink. The jellies are fresh, not too sweet. Later in the summer, other fruits—ripe apricots, nectarines, or peaches—would work well, too. This is a proper jelly, made from scratch, and it's not difficult to do. Banish all thoughts of jello from your mind. It may seem like a lot of gelatin, but alcohol inhibits its setting properties so you need more.

serves 6

for the jellies

16fl oz high-quality sparkling lemonade

⅓ cup granulated sugar

4 broad strips of unwaxed lemon zest, white pith removed, plus the juice of 3 lemons

leaves from a small bunch of mint

⅔oz gelatin leaves (they can be any grade, though I use platinum as it gives a clearer jelly)

16fl oz cava

for the rest

2 cups strawberries

¼ cup superfine sugar

1 tablespoon orange juice

1 teaspoon finely grated orange zest

3 tablespoons sweet or cream sherry

whipped cream or crème fraîche, to serve (optional)

Put the lemonade, sugar, lemon zest, juice, and mint in a saucepan and slowly bring to a boil, stirring a little to help the sugar dissolve. Reduce the heat and simmer for 2 minutes. Remove from the heat and leave it to infuse for about 90 minutes. Strain through a nylon mesh strainer.

Put the gelatin leaves in a bowl and cover with cold water. Leave them to soften for 5 minutes. Pour ½ cup of the lemon liquid into a small saucepan and heat. Once hot, but not boiling, remove this from the heat. Lift the gelatin out of the water, gently squeeze out the excess water, then add it to the warm lemon liquid and stir to dissolve. It's very important that gelatin is never added to very hot liquid, as this destroys its setting properties. Add the remaining lemon liquid and the cava. Transfer to a pitcher, then pour into 6 glasses or cups and put in the fridge to set.

To serve, cut the strawberries into slices about ⅛ inch in thickness; if the strawberries are big, chop them coarsely. Toss in the sugar, orange juice, zest, and sherry and let stand for about 20 minutes. The sugar will dissolve and the fruit will become glossy. Spoon some fruit onto each portion. Serve with whipped cream or crème fraîche, if you like.

summer begins with apricot tart

welcoming the warm months

zucchini, ricotta & pecorino fritters

sea bass crudo with radishes & nasturtiums

marcella hazan's roast chicken with lemon

apricot tart

You don't have to plan a menu from the main course (which is what most people do). Who said you have to start in the middle? Start with whatever course you want and see where that takes you. As new ingredients come into season, there's always something I really want to cook—asparagus, raspberries, apricots—and, every year, dishes I want to make again. Planning a meal starting with a hero dessert, or a favorite salad, gives a different perspective. And who knows where you'll end up?

Even before strawberries have arrived, Italian apricots start appearing in the shops in late spring. Some are uniformly golden in color, others pale and tinged with green. My favorites are those flushed with red and stippled with little brown freckles; in those, you can see summer. They're so lovely in the hand, too, a nice size and weight to conjure with, and they're gone in four bites (though I try to stretch out the pleasure by nibbling).

Apart from a bowl of raspberries with cream, apricot tart is my favorite summer dessert. Even the most unpromising apricots—unripe and dull—seem to become vanilla-sweet and develop a balancing acidity when heat is applied. That's why they're so good with pastry; pastry needs fruit with a little tartness. Apricots aren't simply "sweet" in the way that sugar is, baked apricots really do taste of honey…and can even have a bass note of what distinguishes the best Rieslings: gasoline (in a good way).

As making the tart takes a bit of time, the main course here—chicken with lemon—is incredibly easy, and there is something very pleasing about the simplicity of a roast chicken preceded by an elegant salad and followed by a fruit tart. Two "appetizers" up front might seem like overkill—and you can always jettison one of them—but I like the way this menu weaves around, and the fact that the refined (the fish salad) stands alongside the everyday (the chicken). Some people—cooks and noncooks alike—think that roast chicken isn't special enough for anything other than a family meal, but my heart lifts when I realize it's on the menu in someone else's house. Add lemon, and that turns into proper excitement. These two ingredients, together, have such potential. In this meal the whole fruit—inside the bird—creates lemony juices as it cooks.

The most difficult dish to pull off here—perhaps a little counterintuitively—is actually the salad; you need to judge the dressing and the seasoning well, and be careful not to overwhelm it, so go easy on the flowers. If the tart seems like an effort too far, then bake halved apricots with white wine, vanilla seeds, and sugar, until they're soft and caramelized in patches. Serve with crème fraîche, or whipped cream into which you've stirred some amaretto liqueur. The fruit will be luscious. You won't be starting summer with apricot tart, but at least you'll have apricots.

zucchini, ricotta & pecorino fritters

This is an indulgence, a totally unnecessary course, but the one that everyone will love you for because it's little fried things. Eat these standing around the stove, hot from the skillet. Or, if you want to move things around, serve them as a side to the chicken (that means keeping them warm in a low oven while you eat the fish).

serves 6

6oz fresh ricotta

1lb 2oz zucchini, coarsely shredded on a box grater

2 garlic cloves, very finely sliced

4 scallions, very finely sliced

2 large eggs, lightly beaten

2 teaspoons finely grated unwaxed lemon zest

½ cup finely grated pecorino cheese

sea salt flakes and freshly ground black pepper

¾ cup all-purpose flour

regular olive oil, for frying

lemon wedges, to serve

Put the ricotta into a sieve lined with a piece of cheesecloth, set it over a bowl, and leave it for a couple of hours to allow some of the moisture to drain off.

Put the grated zucchini into another piece of cheesecloth (you'll need to do this in batches) and pull the cloth around them to form a bag. Squeeze out as much of the excess water as possible, really twisting and pressing the bag with your hands, otherwise your fritters will be rather wet. (You'll be amazed at how much water zucchini contain.)

In a large bowl, combine the zucchini, garlic, scallions, ricotta, eggs, lemon zest, pecorino, salt, and pepper. Mash everything together with a fork and add the flour. The mixture should be soft, but not runny.

Line a large baking sheet with paper towels. In a large skillet, heat ½ inch of regular olive oil until you can see it shimmering. Working in batches, add 2 tablespoons of the batter to the hot oil, then spread this out to make a 3-inch fritter. Add 3 or 4 to the skillet at once, but don't overcrowd it. Fry over medium-high heat, turning them over once, until browned and crisp, about 3 minutes in total. Drain the fritters on the paper towels, throw a little salt on top, and serve immediately, with lemon wedges, while you quickly fry the rest. Or keep the cooked fritters warm in a low oven while you finish the cooking and serve them all as soon as the last fritter comes out of the pan.

sea bass crudo with radishes & nasturtiums

Rarely am I as exacting with recipes as I am here, but the proportions in the dressing really are important, as is the quality of all the ingredients. This is a very simple dish, so you need to put it together with care. The flavors—the pepperiness from the nasturtium leaves and radishes, the sweet brininess of the fish—make it pure and visceral. It's like eating summer. Try to find a lemon-flavored extra virgin olive oil (you'll use it for other dishes, too). You can find nasturtium leaves and flowers at some farmer's markets, and online (see page 252). You can make this with fillets of sea bass (branzino), porgy, red snapper, or fluke fillets.

serves 6

for the dressing
⅓ cup extra virgin olive oil, preferably lemon-flavored

1½ tablespoons unseasoned rice vinegar

1½ tablespoons lemon juice

1½ teaspoons liquid honey

3 teaspoons very finely chopped shallots

sea salt flakes and freshly ground black pepper

for the salad
½oz mixed micro greens, such as garden cress, and baby leaves such as pea shoots

1 small bunch of nasturtium flowers and leaves

12 radishes, preferably French breakfast radishes, washed, leaves removed, and long tails cut off

1lb 2oz spanking-fresh sea bass (branzino), porgy, red snapper, or fluke fillets

Make the dressing by putting all the ingredients in a small bowl and whisking with a fork. Set aside for about 15 minutes; the shallots will gently flavor the dressing as it sits.

Pick through the leaves and flowers, choosing the freshest and best-looking specimens. Shave the radishes into thin tear-shaped slices or disks using a mandoline slicer, or cut them very finely with a sharp knife.

Using a sharp, fine-bladed knife (a fish filleting knife is ideal, if you have one), slice the fish fillets thinly across their width, as you would smoked salmon, leaving the skin behind. Lay the fish on a big plate, or divide among 6 smaller plates. Spoon on two-thirds of the dressing.

Scatter the radishes, leaves, and flowers over the top, then spoon on the rest of the dressing. Don't use too many flowers or leaves—just keep them to add to another salad—or the whole thing looks blowsy rather than delicate. Serve immediately.

marcella hazan's roast chicken with lemon

A classic recipe from the great Marcella Hazan, this couldn't be simpler and works every time. I get such a thrill from the way that these very basic ingredients—chicken, lemons, and seasoning—are transformed with no added fat and no fuss, just by heat. Marcella suggests cooking the chicken for twenty minutes per 1lb, but I've reduced that to roughly fifteen minutes per 1lb, plus another fifteen minutes.

serves 6

4½lb chicken (the very best you can afford)

sea salt flakes and freshly ground black pepper

2 small unwaxed lemons

Preheat the oven to 350°F.

Remove the excess fat from around the opening to the cavity of the chicken. Season well inside. Dry the skin of the chicken using paper towels, or the skin on the breast will stick to the pan.

Roll the lemons on your work surface to soften them (I then bash them with a rolling pin, but not so hard that they burst), then prick each fruit all over with a skewer. Put these inside the bird and close the cavity using wooden toothpicks. Tie the legs together, but not tightly (tying them together just stops them widening as the bird cooks, which can tear the skin). Season the outside.

Put the bird into a roasting pan or ovenproof dish—breast-side down—where it can lie without too much room around it (otherwise the juices just evaporate and burn). Roast for 30 minutes, then turn the bird over so the breast is uppermost. Roast for another 30 minutes.

Increase the oven temperature to 400°F and roast for another 15 minutes. The skin should be puffed up and golden and the lemons should have made lovely cooking juices around the bird. Check that the bird is cooked; the juices that run from between the leg and the rest of the body should be clear, with no trace of pink. If there is some pink, cook for a few minutes more, then check again.

Serve whole, carving it at the table and spooning the lemony cooking juices over each helping. It needs only the simplest accompaniments: good bread or little roasted potatoes and a green or tomato salad.

apricot tart

Of all the summer tarts, this is my favorite. Apricots respond so brilliantly to heat—becoming both tarter and more honeyed as they cook—and are one of the best fruits to pair with pastry. The pastry here, which I've stolen from the chef Alastair Little—it's in his book *Italian Kitchen* and it's worth tracking down a used copy if you don't have it—is very easy to use because of his technique.

serves 6 to 8

for the pastry

1½ cups all-purpose flour

¼ cup superfine sugar

⅓ cup ground almonds

sea salt flakes

1½ sticks chilled unsalted butter, chopped

1 medium egg yolk

½ teaspoon amaretto

for the frangipane

3 tablespoons unsalted butter, softened

3 tablespoons superfine sugar

1 large egg, lightly beaten

½ teaspoon amaretto

¼ cup blanched almonds, freshly ground

¼ cup all-purpose flour

for the filling

2¼lb ripe apricots, halved and pitted

¼ cup superfine sugar

⅓ cup sliced almonds

confectioners' sugar, to dust

To make the pastry, blitz the flour, sugar, ground almonds, and a pinch of salt in a food processor for a few seconds. Add the butter and whiz again until the mixture looks like bread crumbs. Add the egg yolk and amaretto. Blend again until the mixture forms a ball. Form this into a salami shape (though be careful not to overwork the pastry), about 2 inches in diameter. Seal in plastic wrap and chill for at least 2 hours.

For the frangipane, beat the butter and sugar until light and creamy. Gradually add the egg, beating well after each addition. Add the amaretto and stir in the almonds and flour.

Almond pastry is difficult to roll out, so don't even try. Just cut the chilled log into slices about ⅛ inch thick. Put these, overlapping, into a loose-bottomed 9-inch tart pan, also lining the sides. Press the pastry into shape, making it as even as possible, with the sides a little thicker than the bottom. Cover with plastic wrap and freeze for about 20 minutes (or put in the coldest part of the fridge), to help stop the pastry from shrinking. Spread the frangipane over the bottom of the tart; it won't look as if there's enough of it, but it puffs up.

Preheat the oven to 350°F.

Toss the apricot halves with the sugar. Lay them, almost vertically and slightly overlapping, on top of the frangipane. They will shrink during cooking. Bake for 30 minutes.

Remove the tart from the oven and reduce the oven temperature to 300°F. Sprinkle with the almonds and dust with confectioners' sugar, then return the tart to the oven for a further 45 minutes.

Let cool to room temperature, then transfer to a plate. Dust with a little more confectioners' sugar. This is best served the day it's made.

take me back to istanbul

little mouthfuls from beside the bosphorus

roast split eggplants with goat cheese

sautéed squid with chile, dill & tahini dressing

lamb kofta

sweet pickled cherries

turkish coffee ice cream

We're dragging our luggage across the lobby when the hotel owner spots my seven-year-old. As we sign the register, he rings the little brass bell that sits on the reception desk and Turkish delight—a sugar-dusted pyramid of it in a stemmed dish—arrives. My son's eyes are so wide with wonder, he might as well have stumbled into the snows of Narnia. This is the kind of warmth you find in Istanbul. It's a big city—the population has grown from two million to fourteen million in the last twenty-five years—but constant acts of kindness make it feel like a village. Spiced apple tea and pastries are delivered to our room and we sit on the tiny terrace, a stone's throw from the Blue Mosque, devouring baklava and blue skies.

Istanbul, for me, is summed up by the color blue. I've only been there under summer skies, never in winter; the only item I bought on my first visit was a blue shawl—the color of the Iznik tiles that decorate so many of Istanbul's interiors—for covering my head when visiting mosques. And then there's the Bosphorus, the blue water dividing and joining the two sides of the city, European and Asian, its two worlds. Blue is an optimistic color, it means horizons and space, skies and seas. I feel, in Istanbul, that I can stretch out my arms and touch the rest of the world. The city is at the edge of everything, and the world also comes to it. Sit in a rickety teahouse by the Bosphorus and you can see it, boats and ferries and tankers from Norway and Italy and Cambodia—even warships from Russia—churning up the water, while smaller vessels bravely steer a course among them (ship counting and serious shipwatching are Istanbul pastimes).

The food here is at the meeting point of lots of cultures, too. On the surface it seems simple; most meals start with vegetables, cucumbers as juicy and taut as apples, firm chilled radishes, slices of scarlet bell pepper. The counterpoints to these are tart or salty, the snow-white cheese *beyaz peynir*, clouds of pale creamy-pink tarama, bowls of thick yogurt. The tarama is a dish shared with the Balkans and Greece. But look beyond these; *acuka*, a purée of red bell peppers, walnuts, garlic, tomato and chile, is Syrian in origin; the chicken coated with a creamy walnut and garlic sauce is from Circassia; *manti*, little dumplings stuffed with spiced lamb and smothered in yogurt, are thought to have come to Turkey along the Silk Road from Central Asia. There are influences from all over the former Ottoman Empire: the Middle East, the Balkans, the Caucasus, and parts of North Africa.

You think you know, or have at least read about, all the preparations for eggplant and lamb, and then you visit Çiya Sofrası in Kadıköy, probably the best and most-loved restaurant on the Asian shore, and one that has been described as "a garden of lost cultures and forgotten tastes." Here the owner, Musa Daðdeviren, is trying to document, restore, and maintain Turkish dishes that could otherwise get left behind; you don't recognize many of them, neither the cold mezze on one side of the restaurant, nor the contents of the bubbling pots on the other (and my Istanbullu friends tell me it's often the same for them). Much of the food is in shades of deep purple or green: lamb with plums, melting eggplants slick with pomegranate molasses, pilaf with mulberries, fat glossy stuffed vine leaves. You choose your mezze and pay for the plate by weight, take it to your table and try to work out which flavors—cumin, sumac, or *pul biber*—are playing across one another. There are some ingredients, though—milk thistle, hyssop—that you probably won't guess correctly.

Food is taken very seriously in Istanbul, but not because it's cool. Offering people good food is a tenet of faith (it's a command of the Prophet) even among those who hold none. Its importance was signaled from the earliest days of the Ottoman Empire. When Sultan Mehmet II conquered Constantinople in the 15th century he built the Topkapı Palace with a huge four-domed kitchen. More domes and sections were added until the kitchens, at their peak (when feeding guests and visiting diplomats), housed nearly 1,400 cooks. It was a furnace of culinary creativity where new dishes were developed, Byzantine recipes were adopted and updated, and ingredients from every part of the Empire were used. Imagine the discussions, the excitement when chiles arrived, or unfamiliar varieties of grape. Cooking was respected, considered an art; poets and musicians composed poems and sang songs about it and every wealthy household in the city tried to keep up with the standards set in the Topkapı.

The Palace kitchens were separated into specialized sections—pastry, milk puddings, halvah, drinks, even pickles—and when Turkey became a secular Republic in 1923 the cooks lost their jobs. Many of them went abroad, but the idea of specialties continued. In markets today you can see picklers and preservers, their green figs and pink-tinged florets of cauliflower glowing behind glass, and the *muhallebicisi*, or "milk-pudding makers" (the very idea of being a milk-pudding maker, provider of sweetness and comfort) have small, simple restaurants (though most now sell pastries and other snacks as well as milk puddings). In these you can have *muhallebi*, soft, just-set squares of milk pudding made with rice flour, *tavukgöğsü*, an ancient dish of poached chicken breast pounded with milk, rice flour, sugar, and cinnamon, and *aşure*, a wheat pudding made with nuts and dried fruits. These dishes are often fragrant with mastic, a translucent resin that tastes slightly of pine and cedar, or flower waters. What is so seductive about the food in Istanbul is the blending—an accident of history—of simple nomadic dishes and staples with the remnants of the more sophisticated palace cuisine. It's rich and layered and there's a place to eat every kind of food at all different times of the day. There are rooftop cocktail bars with glittering views; *kebapçı*, where you can spend half an hour trying to choose which of twenty-five kebabs you're going to order; or street food stands that lure you with the charred oiliness of mackerel and the slightly sweet smell of *simit*, sesame-flecked bracelets of bread.

Turks love a big breakfast: vegetables, cheese, figs, and watermelon along with preserves, yogurt, and honey, which is a mere precursor to mid-morning coffee. Then there's lunch, taken in one of the many *lokantas* (simple taverns or "canteens"). As late afternoon approaches, I wonder if I'll have pastries and tea, or *şerbet* (sweet cordials made from mint, sour cherries, quinces, or lemons) or ice cream. I check every ice cream shop I see, looking for the unusual, mulberry or tahini, though I can always depend on a little tub of rose ice cream flavored with *salep*, dried and ground orchid root. Then it's mezze and raki before dinner.

The Turkish novelist Orhan Pamuk has written about *hüzün*, the melancholy (which can be painful, but also enjoyable, because it is shared) that he and other Istanbullus feel. It might be engendered simply by rain on a window, or the sad weak light that gathers at the end of a winter afternoon. But *hüzün* is also a sense of loss, the result of being born into a city "buried under the ashes of a ruined empire." I do not feel this melancholy. It is not mine to feel. If I'm in Istanbul during Ramadan, when the area around the Blue Mosque is full of picnickers spreading out cloths on the ground and hungrily eating *börek* and *lahmacun* at midnight, I can't even see it. I just see generosity and beauty and joy.

I used to play a game, when I first started traveling in my late teens. I would ask myself "Could you live here if you had to?" I was testing my independence. I have never stopped playing this game. The first time I rode the ferry from one side of the Bosphorus to the other, going to the Asian shore with the end-of-day commuters—talking loudly, eating peaches, reading—I watched the water become a great white spume behind the boat and asked myself this question. I looked at the skyline with its domes and rocketlike minarets, its mix of old and modern, and thought, oh yes. But I want an apartment with a view, however small a fragment, of the blue Bosphorus, and a good café nearby where I can start every day with salty cheese and melon.

roast split eggplants with goat cheese

This is one of the simplest recipes in the book, but the combination of temperatures and flavors—slightly smoky eggplant, rich oil, tangy goat cheese, and citrussy sumac—is perfect. I often eat this just on its own. Use a good extra virgin olive oil, a bottle that you really love. Its flavor is central.

serves 6

6 medium eggplants

sea salt flakes and freshly ground black pepper

extra virgin olive oil

10½oz soft mild goat cheese, or goat curd

a little sumac

Preheat the oven to 375°F and put a baking sheet inside to heat up. Wash the eggplants and lay them on the hot sheet. Roast for 45 minutes to 1 hour. They should be completely tender right through.

Split each eggplant down the middle so that it opens out. Season the insides, drizzle with extra virgin olive oil, then spoon some of the goat cheese or curd inside. Sprinkle with a little more extra virgin olive oil, then some sumac, and serve immediately.

sautéed squid with chile, dill & tahini dressing

The squid here can be served warm rather than piping hot, so you can, in theory, cook it just before your guests arrive, if you prefer not to do it when they're there. There's not much to this dish—charred squid, chile, tahini, dill—but the flavors contrast well. You get to eat all the smells that drift past you as you stroll around Istanbul.

serves 6

for the tahini dressing
¼ cup tahini

2 small garlic cloves, finely grated

2 tablespoons plain Greek or Turkish yogurt

2 tablespoons extra virgin olive oil

juice of ½ lemon

sea salt flakes and freshly ground black pepper

for the squid
2lb squid, small if you can get them (cleaned weight)

regular olive oil

juice of ½ lemon, plus lemon wedges, to serve

2 red chiles, halved, seeded, and shredded

1 green chile, halved, seeded, and shredded

¾oz bunch of dill, leaves coarsely chopped

4oz baby spinach leaves

To make the dressing, whisk together the tahini, garlic, yogurt, and extra virgin olive oil. Whisk in the lemon juice until the dressing is smooth—tahini tends to seize when you add anything acidic—then add 3 tablespoons of water and seasoning. The mixture should be slightly thicker than heavy cream, no thicker, so add more water if you need to. Check the seasoning. Cover and put in the fridge. If you're making this ahead of time, you need to take it out of the fridge well before you want to serve it, as the cold will make the dressing firm up.

Wash the squid, removing any whitish stuff from their insides, and pat dry on paper towels (if they're wet they won't take on a good color while they're cooking). If the squid are small, leave them whole. If they're larger, cut off the wings and set them aside with the tentacles. Cut the bodies down one side to open them out. Halve lengthwise and score the inside of the flesh with a cross-hatch pattern, without cutting all the way through.

Put the squid into a bowl with enough regular olive oil to just moisten the pieces.

Heat a skillet until really hot. Season the squid and cook it in batches, pressing down a little on the pieces as they fry. Small squid only need about 30 seconds on each side to become golden and cooked. Season as you go. As each batch is ready, remove it to a warmed plate and squeeze lemon juice over it. Once all the squid is cooked, add a little more oil to the pan and cook the chiles for 20 seconds or so, then toss them into the squid. Add the dill and baby spinach and toss (the leaves will wilt). Put on a big platter, and serve the tahini dressing on the side with lemon wedges.

lamb kofta

Kofta seem easy—they're just meatballs, after all—but the texture and their seasoning are really important. Pummel the meat and the other ingredients with your hands to mix everything well, then fry and taste a little nugget of the meat—so you can safely judge the spicing and seasoning—before cooking the whole lot.

serves 6

1 onion

⅔ cup flat-leaf parsley leaves

⅓ cup mint leaves

2¼lb finely ground lamb shoulder

2 garlic cloves, finely grated

1½ teaspoons ground cumin

1½ teaspoons ground cinnamon

1½ teaspoons ground allspice

½ teaspoon grated nutmeg

1½ teaspoons sea salt flakes, or to taste

lots of freshly ground black pepper

regular olive oil, for frying

Grate the onion coarsely. Put it in a strainer set over a bowl and squeeze out most of the liquid by pressing on the pulp, using the back of a wooden spoon, or your fists. Put the onion into a large bowl. Finely chop the parsley and mint and add them, too. Mix in the meat, garlic, spices, and salt and pepper until thoroughly combined; using your hands is the best way.

Place a little regular olive oil in a skillet and add a small nugget of the meat mixture, frying on both sides, until browned. Taste for seasoning and spicing, then adjust the raw meat mixture as required.

Shape into patties or meatballs, or mold around flat skewers. Cover and let chill in the fridge for about 1 hour (this helps them firm up).

Brush a griddle pan with regular olive oil if you are cooking flat skewers, or add a couple of tablespoons to a skillet if you are cooking meatballs. Cook the kofta until golden brown all over and cooked the way you like them (they don't have to be cooked right through, and they can be served rare). You need a good color all over the surfaces of the kofta.

Eat with flatbreads or a grain dish (bulgur or rice), a bowl of Greek yogurt, and the pickled cherries on the following page.

sweet pickled cherries

Not really Turkish at all, but French—*cerises au vinaigre*—these work brilliantly with lamb, yogurt, and goat cheese, so they're perfect with this meal, and make it special. It's better if you prepare these cherries a little in advance—a week, if possible—though I've often just made them the day before I want to serve them. Packed in a sterilized jar (see below) with a non-reactive lid, they will keep for a few years.

fills a 1-quart jar

1lb 2oz sweet cherries

1⅓ cups white wine vinegar

2¼ cups granulated sugar

½ cinnamon stick

6 black peppercorns

2 cloves

Prick each cherry with a skewer or darning needle (this stops them from bursting), but keep the stalks on if you can, as they look good.

Heat the vinegar with the sugar and spices, stirring a little to help the sugar dissolve.

Add the cherries to the mixture and simmer gently for 4 minutes. Lift the cherries out with a slotted spoon into a clean, warm jar (if you plan to keep these rather than use them all for this meal, you should use a sterilized jar, see below). Jars should have non-reactive lids.

Remove the spices and boil the vinegar liquid until it becomes slightly syrupy; it will thicken more as it cools. Once cool, pour it over the cherries, leaving an inch or so of space above the level of the liquid and the top of the jar. Screw on the lid.

to sterilize jars

Put the jars and lids through the dishwasher and use while both are still hot, or wash them in soapy water, then dry in a low oven for 30 minutes.

turkish coffee ice cream

This is not a Turkish recipe, but an ice cream inspired by the flavors of the thick coffee you're served in Istanbul. It's the simplest ice cream I make: mix and freeze.

makes about 1 pint

2 tablespoons instant espresso powder

ground seeds from 10 green cardamom pods

1¼ cups heavy cream

¾ cup sweetened condensed milk

Mix the coffee, 2 tablespoons of boiling water, and the ground cardamom together. Let cool.

Beat the cream and condensed milk together using an electric hand mixer until the mixture is quite thick, then stir in the spiced coffee.

Scrape into a container, cover with plastic wrap or a lid, and freeze. The ice cream doesn't need to be churned. It does becomes very firm, however, so you need to take it out of the freezer about 20 minutes before you want to serve it.

crabs walk sideways

a feast of shellfish

rye bread with radish butter & salmon caviar

crab with potatoes & home-made mayonnaise

fresh raspberry lemonade

strawberry & buttermilk ice cream

Sometimes meals aren't just about eating…they are events. Take the Provençal *grand aïoli*, that feast of poached salt cod, vegetables, and garlicky mayo, eaten—with the obligatory rosé wine—in the garden; or cook big pots of *moules marinières* for friends and watch how they behave. That dish makes everyone act as if they're on vacation. It's not just the taste, it's the fact that you have to eat with your hands, actively digging out the mussel flesh, and that you get messy. Then—and I think this is key—you carelessly throw the shells aside. You can't not relax when you're nonchalantly throwing food around. If you're eating these meals outside, where your tastebuds seem to be on high alert, everything tastes better, too.

A crab feast—because you usually only get it at the seaside—is another eventlike meal, and it's surprisingly easy to pull off. Cover your table with paper, buy a loaf of good sourdough, and make your own mayonnaise. Boil small waxy potatoes (they're not obligatory, as you have bread, but some people prefer them) and toss a big green salad (which should be dressed lightly, because you're also having mayonnaise). Provide lemon wedges and bottles of cold flinty white wine.

If you don't have all the proper paraphernalia for crab eating, ask friends to bring nutcrackers and skewers, though I've resorted to using rolling pins in the past. Ice cream follows this crab feast, but you could serve raspberries or strawberries and cream instead. I like the salty fishiness of salmon caviar to start, but something as simple as radishes, good butter, and baguettes with flaked sea salt would also be good.

The highlight of the meal is the crab. As people compete over who can get the most meat out of the spindly legs, the table is soon covered in bits of pinky-brown shrapnel, squeezed lemon wedges, crumpled napkins, and corks. The smell of the sea hovers over the table. Another bottle of wine is opened and people decide to stay "just a little bit longer."

If you really don't want to do your own, you can buy cooked crab from your fish market (but you do need a *good* fish market for this). Either way, if you've never taken a crab apart before—and have always eaten cracked crab—you need to check out how to guide your guests through it. Imagine a table full of hungry people who have no idea how to extract the sweet, briny meat…. It is up to you how much you prepare the crabs once they've been cooked. I've included instructions for how to deconstruct a crab completely, but all you absolutely have to do is separate the body and the back shell and remove the gills and the stomach sacs. All the hammering and cracking can be done with your guests.

This feast doesn't have to be lifestyle-magazine perfect, in fact the more do-it-yourself it is the better. I use a wallpaper table (bought from a home renovation store and kept in the shed) for this kind of meal, and put tealight candles in jam jars. Just make sure you have a huge bowl for the crab debris and plenty of finger bowls for dipping fishy fingers. Things will get messy.

rye bread with radish butter & salmon caviar

Peppery, earthy, salty: a good way to whet the appetite.

serves 8

9oz red radishes, preferably
French breakfast radishes,
trimmed

1 stick unsalted butter,
completely softened

½ teaspoon sea salt flakes

freshly ground white or
black pepper

loaf of firm rye bread

3½oz jar of salmon caviar

Put the radishes in the bowl of a food processor and pulse 4 to 5 times until chopped very fine. Transfer to a piece of cheesecloth and wring out the excess liquid with your hands.

Put into a bowl and add the butter. With a rubber spatula, work the radishes and butter with the salt until the mixture comes together into a smooth, pliable mass. Put the mixture into a ramekin or bowl and grind some pepper over the top. The butter will keep, covered with plastic wrap, in the fridge for a couple of days. Remove it 15 minutes before serving, to let it soften.

Spread the radish butter on small squares of rye bread and spoon salmon caviar on top.

crab with potatoes & homemade mayonnaise

Make sure all the ingredients for the mayonnaise are at room temperature and that the eggs are fresh. If it looks as though the mayonnaise is going to break at any point, add 1 to 2 tablespoons of warm water and beat like crazy. If this doesn't rescue it, start with a fresh egg yolk, a little salt, and a smidgen of mustard and slowly beat the broken mixture into this. It should come together. Mayonnaise is all about seasoning, so taste and taste until you get it right, adding more vinegar or even a squeeze of lemon juice if it needs it. There are videos online about how to prepare crab after cooking it, so find one and use it as extra help if you need to.

serves 8

for the mayonnaise

2 medium egg yolks

½ teaspoon Dijon mustard

1 tablespoon white wine vinegar

⅔ cup mild-tasting extra virgin olive oil (mild and fruity, not a grassy Tuscan oil)

⅔ cup sunflower oil

sea salt flakes and freshly ground white pepper

lemon juice, to taste (optional)

for the crabs

6 to 8 x 2lb live Dungeness crabs, or 4 dozen live blue crabs

1¾lb new, soft-skinned potatoes

about 8 mint sprigs

sourdough bread, to serve

Start with the mayonnaise. In a bowl, mix the egg yolks with the mustard and half the vinegar. Beating all the time with a wooden spoon, or using an electric hand mixer, start adding the oils very slowly, drop by drop. (You can also make this in a food processor, but I can never be bothered to get that out just for mayonnaise.) Wait until each drop of oil is well amalgamated and the mixture has thickened before adding the next. Once you have a thick mixture, add the rest of the vinegar and season. Taste to see whether you need more salt or some lemon juice. If you make this in advance, and so have to keep it in the fridge, you might find that it separates slightly. If this happens, let stand until nearly room temperature, then beat in a little warm water.

Kill the crabs humanely (look online for details). Put in 2 large pots, each containing 5 quarts of cold water, and add plenty of salt. Bring to a boil and then let simmer for 15 minutes for Dungeness crabs, or 10 minutes for blue crabs. Remove from the water and let cool.

To clean the crabs, pull off the "aprons" on the undersides, then break off the back shells (for Dungeness crabs, you may need a knife to help with this). Discard the back shells and their contents. Pull off the gills ("dead men's fingers"), mandibles, and any greenish or orange matter from the bodies, and discard. Rinse the crab bodies, then snap each body in half. (The photographs opposite and overleaf show European brown crabs, which are not shelled or halved before serving.)

Scrub some of the skin off the potatoes and boil them with the mint until tender. Drain and put into a warmed serving bowl.

Serve the crabs with the potatoes, mayonnaise, and sourdough bread. You'll only need to add a green salad, claw crackers, and crab picks.

fresh raspberry lemonade

An extra for this meal, but good to make, especially if there are going to be children among the party. Pure, intense raspberry joy.

makes a generous 1 quart

1lb raspberries

½ cup superfine sugar, divided, plus more to taste

finely grated zest and juice of 4 unwaxed lemons

1 quart cold sparkling water

ice cubes, to serve

Toss the raspberries in a bowl with ¼ cup of the sugar and let stand for 1 hour.

Purée the raspberries with the rest of the sugar in a food processor (not a blender as they crush the seeds, making the mixture bitter). Push the resulting purée through a nylon mesh strainer (the acidity of the raspberries would react with a wire mesh strainer or metal sieve).

Mix the purée with the lemon zest and juice and the sparkling water. Check to see whether you need to add any more sugar, as this will depend on how tart your fruit was. Serve in chilled glasses over ice.

strawberry & buttermilk ice cream

No custard, no heat, this is an easy ice cream to make. It also has a lovely texture, like sherbet.

makes 1 quart

1lb 2oz strawberries

scant 1 cup superfine sugar

1 vanilla bean, split lengthwise

1¾ cups buttermilk

½ cup sour cream

pinch of sea salt flakes

Hull and slice the strawberries and put them into a bowl with half the sugar and the seeds from the vanilla bean (scrape out the seeds using the tip of a knife). Let stand for about 30 minutes. The strawberries will become soft and exude some juice.

Transfer the fruit with all the juice and the rest of the sugar to a food processor and whiz to a purée. Push the purée through a nylon mesh strainer to get rid of the seeds. Mix with the buttermilk, sour cream, and salt.

Churn in an ice-cream machine, or transfer to a shallow container and put in the freezer. If you're using the manual method, take the ice cream out and churn it—either using an electric hand mixer or by putting the mixture in a food processor—3 times during the freezing process. Do this first after about 1 hour, when the mixture is setting around the edges, then at 2-hour intervals. Cover with a lid, or with plastic wrap or greaseproof paper, between each churning, and when you store it.

Take the ice cream out of the freezer about 10 minutes before you want to serve it, to allow it to soften slightly.

too hot to cook

for when the temperature soars

beets & carrots with cumin & haydari

roast tomatoes, fennel & chickpeas with preserved lemons & honey

cherries in wine with cardamom cream & rose pistachio shortbread

Summer cooking is weighed down by fantasy. We imagine going to the market with our battered-but-much-loved basket and filling it with zucchini flowers that we'll stuff and deep-fry for adoring guests. But nobody does this once the temperature is nudging the mid-eighties. This is not the time for making complicated food. Heat slows the brain. Our appetites are fickle as well; we aren't sure what we want to eat. Even the most enthusiastic cooks have days when a tomato salad is the most they can muster (and there's nothing wrong with that; it's one of the best dishes of the summer).

On the other hand, you want to give friends something they aren't making for themselves at home (so *not* that tomato salad). What do I crave in the heat? Yogurt and cucumbers straight from the fridge, vegetables with varying textures—I want the crunch of radishes, the softness of roast tomatoes—the piney breeze of dill, food I can pick at, rather than a plateful I feel I have to eat.

You need to put the oven on for this meal, but the cooking isn't taxing. The only thing you have to do for the appetizer is to briefly sauté the vegetables (to help them take on the flavor of the cumin seeds); beyond that you just have to prepare the yogurt. This is a very cooling dish.

The main course only requires you to shove two roasting pans in the oven (and this can be done the day before). I've suggested serving couscous, but Arab flatbread would be fine instead.

You can dispense with the shortbread if that makes things easier (and cooler) and only serve the cherries with the cream. Alternatively, if it's really hot, simply offer fresh cherries, along with slices of melon, seeds removed, on ice. I've had this in Greece and was as eager to get my hands on the ice as on the cherries.

To drink, either make a big pitcher of *citron pressé*, or (so that people can adjust the acidity and sweetness themselves), put a pitcher of lemon juice, another of simple sugar syrup, and a third (big) pitcher of iced water on the table. (To make sugar syrup, just mix two parts of granulated sugar to one part of boiling water in a saucepan and stir over medium heat until the sugar has dissolved, then let cool.) Alternatively, make a hibiscus-flavored syrup (see page 242) and adjust the sweetness by adding more water or more citrus juice (you can use lemon juice; you don't have to use lime). Ice-cold hibiscus—it's drunk in the Middle East and Mexico—with its taste of tart berries, is really thirst-quenching and a gorgeous color. A special drink isn't necessary, though. Iced water is enough.

It's a good idea to make most of the food the day before. In the summer I often cook late at night, the windows and door of the kitchen open so I can catch the breeze. It's cooler, you're not under pressure, and you can get a shock of coldness by standing in the open door of the freezer from time to time. If you're lucky—or simply organized—you'll have a stash of granita or sorbet in there, too. When the cooking is done, you can eat a bowlful of it in the garden, big mouthfuls of fruity shards of ice, in the dark. Cook's perk.

beets & carrots with cumin & haydari

Haydari is a mixture of strained yogurt, herbs, and garlic. I like chile in it, too, as that way you get some heat against the coolness of yogurt. It's a bit of a pain to cut the carrots into matchsticks, but it's the only taxing thing about this recipe. You can roast the beets yourself, but you're not supposed to be doing much cooking here, so buying ready-cooked beets (or vacuum-packed cooked beets)—as long as they're not pickled—is fine.

serves 6

14oz Greek yogurt

extra virgin olive oil

½oz bunch of dill, leaves only, coarsely chopped, divided

2 garlic cloves, crushed

1 red and 1 green chile, halved, seeded, and very finely chopped

sea salt flakes and freshly ground black pepper

1¾lb carrots

1lb 5oz cooked beets

2 teaspoons cumin seeds

½ tablespoon white balsamic vinegar

½ lemon

¼ cup walnut pieces, lightly toasted

Start this dish 2 hours before you want to serve it. Line a sieve with a piece of cheesecloth and set over a bowl. Pour the yogurt into this and let stand a couple of hours. It doesn't need to get that much thicker. Put the strained yogurt into a bowl and add 2 tablespoons of extra virgin olive oil, most of the chopped dill, the garlic, chiles, and seasoning. Don't overmix; you should be able to see flecks of chile.

Peel and cut the carrots into matchsticks. They don't have to be very neat. Cut the beets into slim wedges.

Heat 2 tablespoons extra virgin oil in a large skillet over medium heat. Add half the cumin seeds and allow them to cook for about 30 seconds, then add the carrots. Stir-fry the carrots for about 1 minute: they need to lose their rawness, but still retain crispness so they contrast with the soft beets. Add the white balsamic vinegar, a generous squeeze of lemon juice, and seasoning. Quickly transfer to a bowl.

Add another ½ tablespoon of extra virgin olive oil to the skillet with the rest of the cumin seeds. Cook for 30 seconds, then add the beets. All you want to do is get them flavored with the cumin and heated through a little; they don't have to be hot. Squeeze on some lemon juice and season.

Put some of the haydari on each of 6 plates, flattening it and swirling it with the back of a spoon. Spoon some beets on top, then some carrots. Scatter with the remaining dill and the walnuts, splash with a little more extra virgin olive oil, and serve.

roast tomatoes, fennel & chickpeas with preserved lemons & honey

It might seem a hassle to roast the fennel and tomatoes separately, but it does make things easier when you come to assemble this, as each element stays intact and keeps its shape. You can use flat-leaf parsley or mint leaves instead of cilantro in the dressing, or extend the dish by adding salad greens (arugula, watercress, or baby spinach) if you like, though then you'll need to make a bit more dressing. You can make all the elements ahead of time. Serve with saffron couscous—it's a great contrast in both color and texture—or flatbread.

serves 6

for the tomatoes
10 large plum tomatoes
3 tablespoons regular olive oil
1 tablespoon balsamic vinegar
1½ tablespoons harissa
2 teaspoons superfine sugar
sea salt flakes and freshly ground black pepper

for the fennel
2 large fennel bulbs
juice of ½ lemon
2 garlic cloves, crushed
½ teaspoon fennel seeds, coarsely crushed in a mortar
generous pinch of crushed red pepper
2½ tablespoons extra virgin olive oil
15oz can of chickpeas, drained and rinsed

for the dressing
2 small preserved lemons, plus 2 teaspoons juice from the jar
2 tablespoons white wine vinegar
1½ tablespoons liquid honey
⅓ cup extra virgin olive oil
¼ cup chopped cilantro

Preheat the oven to 375°F.

Halve the tomatoes lengthwise and lay in a single layer in a roasting pan or ovenproof dish. Mix the regular olive oil, balsamic vinegar, and harissa and pour this over the tomatoes, tossing to coat well, then turn the tomatoes cut-side up. Sprinkle with the sugar and season.

Quarter the fennel bulbs, cut off the stalks, and remove any coarse outer leaves. Pull off any tender fronds (reserve these) and cut each piece of fennel into 1-inch thick wedges, keeping them intact at the base. Toss in a bowl with the lemon juice (it stops them from discoloring). Add the garlic, fennel seeds, chile, and extra virgin olive oil, then season and turn everything over with your hands. Spread out the fennel in a second roasting pan and cover tightly with foil.

Put both pans in the oven. Roast the fennel for 25 to 30 minutes, until tender (the undersides should be pale gold), then remove the foil and roast for another 5 to 10 minutes, or until soft, golden, and slightly charred. Roast the tomatoes for 35 to 40 minutes, or until caramelized in patches and slightly shrunken. Stir the chickpeas into the fennel and taste for seasoning. Let both cool to room temperature.

Now make the dressing. Discard the flesh from the preserved lemons and cut the rind into dice. Whisk the wine vinegar with the preserved lemon juice, honey, and extra virgin olive oil, season, and add the lemon rind and cilantro. Taste for seasoning and sweet-sour balance.

Arrange the fennel, chickpeas, and tomatoes on a platter, adding all the juices from the roasting pans; there might be quite a lot from the tomatoes. Scatter any fennel fronds you reserved over the top. Spoon on the dressing, or serve it on the side.

cherries in wine with cardamom cream & rose pistachio shortbread

Make the cherries the day before and serve them chilled. The cherries can be pitted or unpitted: unpitted looks better (and is less hassle for the cook); pitted is easier for eaters.

serves 6

for the cherries

1¼ cups granulated sugar

2¼ cups Valpolicella, Pinot Noir, or other cherryish red wine

2 broad strips of unwaxed lemon zest

2lb sweet or sour cherries

3 tablespoons kirsch (optional)

squeeze of lemon juice (optional)

for the shortbread

1⅔ sticks unsalted butter, slightly softened

⅔ cup confectioners' sugar, plus more to serve, plus more for the cream

pinch of sea salt flakes

finely grated zest of 1 unwaxed lemon

1½ cups all-purpose flour, plus more to dust

⅔ cup cornstarch

1 teaspoon rose water

1 medium egg, lightly beaten

½ cup shelled unsalted pistachios, chopped

candied rose petals (optional)

for the cream

seeds from 4 green cardamom pods

1¼ cups heavy cream

Put the sugar for the cherries into a large saucepan with the wine, a scant cup of water, and the strips of lemon zest. Bring to a boil, stirring to help the sugar dissolve, then boil for 8 minutes. Reduce the heat, add the cherries, and let simmer for 4 minutes. Lift the cherries out with a slotted spoon onto a tray with a rim or a baking pan; they will stop cooking if they're not touching one another.

Let the syrup cool, then taste and add a slug of kirsch if you want to, or a good squeeze of lemon juice; sometimes the syrup needs this to cut the sugar a bit, but it depends how sweet your cherries are. Put the cherries in a bowl and pour over the red wine syrup.

To make the cookies, beat the butter and confectioner's sugar until creamy, then add the salt and zest. With the mixer on low speed, add the flour, cornstarch, and rose water and beat them together. Remove the dough from the mixer and, on a lightly floured surface, shape it into a log about 2½ inches in diameter. Brush with beaten egg, then roll it in the pistachios. Carefully wrap in foil and chill for 1 hour or so.

Preheat the oven to 350°F. Cut the log into cookies about ⅛ inch thick and arrange them 1 inch apart on cookie sheets. Bake for 15 minutes— they will just turn a little golden around the edges—then let cool for 10 minutes. Carefully lift them onto a wire rack with a metal spatula: they are very fragile, so be careful. Before serving, sift a little confectioners' sugar over the top and scatter with some candied rose petals, if you like.

Grind the cardamom seeds in a mortar and pestle, or in a spice mill. Put the cream into a bowl, add the cardamom, then whip the cream to soft peaks, adding confectioners' sugar to taste.

Serve the cherries with the shortbread and cardamom cream.

how to eat a peach

an elegant summer dinner

summer sandal

crostini with crushed fava beans & 'nduja

melon and goat cheese with red wine & lavender dressing

roast whole fish with fennel & anise aïoli | *tomates provençales aux anchois*

white peaches in chilled moscato

The starring role here goes to the dish that gave this book its name. And it's barely a "dish" at all. I was in my early twenties and in Italy for the first time. I loved not just the food but the attitude to it. It was just so joyful. Every day I shopped, taking Marcella Hazan with me (in book form); every evening I cooked in our tiny vacation rental apartment. Italian cooking is built on good, simple ingredients (firmly regional, with lots of vegetables and pulses) and democratic, in that most people can afford it. The cooking is uncomplicated, too, though its success depends on care and tasting, tasting, tasting.

In an outdoor restaurant on our last night, diners at a neighboring table were given a bowl of peaches for dessert. They halved, pitted, and sliced them, dropped the fruit into glasses, and added cold moscato. They left them to macerate for a while. Then they ate the slices, now flavored with the wine, and drank the wine, now imbued with the peaches. I didn't just think this was a great idea (though it is), I was bowled over that something this simple was considered as desirable as a slaved-over bit of pâtisserie.

In planning this meal, I started with those peaches and worked backward. It is an elegant dinner, a bit Provençal, a bit Italian. The dessert requires no cooking; the fish just goes into the oven where it bakes, same with the tomatoes. The aïoli should be made in advance and left, covered, in the fridge.

You can shed either of the first courses; it depends how much effort you want to make. The melon takes hardly any time, but the crostini do (it's often small things, "bites" to have with drinks, that are demanding). Don't forget the summer sandal, though. It's an indulgent, "height of summer" drink, the kind that makes you want to kick off your shoes to feel cool grass and warm stones under your feet.

summer sandal

This isn't too sweet, though I do have a sweet tooth, so use more or less sugar depending on your taste. I don't add the vodka or Cointreau to the raspberry purée; that way, if you have children around, you can give them glasses of the purée topped off with sparkling lemonade.

makes 6 to 8

½ to ¾ cup confectioners' sugar, to taste

juice of 1 lemon

1lb raspberries

¾ cup freshly squeezed orange juice

6 to 8 tablespoons vodka, divided

6 to 8 tablespoons Cointreau, divided

1 bottle of very cold sparkling white wine

Put the confectioners' sugar, lemon juice, and raspberries into a food processor and whiz to a purée. Push this through a nylon mesh strainer (you don't want the seeds). Add the orange juice to the purée.

Divide the purée between 6 to 8 glasses and add 1 tablespoon of vodka and 1 tablespoon of Cointreau to each. Top off with the sparkling wine to serve, adding it slowly as it will froth.

crostini with crushed fava beans & 'nduja

'Nduja is a spicy Calabrian paste, rather like a soft, spreadable chorizo, but spicier, and without the smoky flavor. You don't need to cook it before using it. Peas can be used instead of fava beans here.

serves 6

2½ cups fresh podded fava beans

2 small garlic cloves,
1 finely chopped, 1 left whole

1 tablespoon lemon juice

2 teaspoons white balsamic vinegar

8 mint leaves, torn

¼ cup extra virgin olive oil, plus more for the crostini

sea salt flakes and freshly ground black pepper

6 medium slices of sourdough bread, or 12 slices of a smaller loaf, such as ciabatta

3½oz 'nduja, broken into little chunks

Preheat the oven to 400°F.

Cook the fava beans in boiling water until tender, about 4 minutes. Drain, then rinse under cold water. When they're cool enough to handle, slip off the skins. Put the bright green kernels in a food processor with the chopped garlic clove, lemon juice, white balsamic vinegar, mint, and extra virgin olive oil, and season with salt and pepper. Pulse until you have a coarse mash. Taste for seasoning and adjust if necessary.

Put the slices of bread on cookie sheets and bake for 10 minutes. The bread should turn pale gold—keep an eye on it so it doesn't go too far—but you won't have to turn the pieces over.

Slice the remaining whole garlic clove in half and lightly rub it over the slices of bread, then sprinkle each piece with a little extra virgin olive oil. Spoon the mashed fava beans onto the toasted bread, then carefully place a few chunks of 'nduja on top of each.

melon and goat cheese with red wine & lavender dressing

This is quite unusual, as the melon is dressed with infused red wine, then finished with olive oil. Basil and mint work, as well as lavender, and prosciutto can be used instead of the cheese. It's a very good example of plain ingredients—melon, cheese—elevated by a bit of thought, rather than by a complicated process.

serves 6

2 lavender sprigs

scant 1 cup red wine

3 tablespoons lavender honey, or regular honey

1 tablespoon good-quality white or red wine vinegar

2 small, ripe, perfumed melons (Cantaloupe)

13oz soft goat cheese

sea salt flakes and freshly ground black pepper

fruity extra virgin olive oil

Put the lavender in a cup or heatproof pitcher. Heat the wine in a saucepan with the honey and vinegar, stirring until the honey melts. Pour it over the lavender. Season with sea salt flakes and freshly ground black pepper and let cool.

Halve the melons and scoop out the seeds, cut into slices, and peel each piece. Put these onto 6 plates or 1 platter. Spoon on the dressing, leaving behind the lavender.

Break up the goat cheese and dot it among the slices of melon. Season, then sprinkle with the extra virgin olive oil.

roast whole fish with fennel & anise aïoli

I don't like drinking Pernod—though I've tried my best—but fennel is a different matter. I can't get enough of it. Here, fennel mayonnaise is piqued with a little drop of Pernod (it's important not to use too much) and is transformed from good to brilliant. I make this with sea bass—you get big sea bass in Great Britain—but use whatever fish you have where you live. This is a great dish to serve to friends as it pretty much looks after itself once it's in the oven.

serves 6

for the fish

1 whole sea bass (branzino), 5½ to 6lb, scaled, gutted, and trimmed, or whole red snapper, redfish, or black sea bass, whatever is available where you live

2 large fennel bulbs

2 tablespoons lemon juice

2 garlic cloves, crushed

1 tablespoon fennel seeds, toasted in a dry skillet and crushed

regular olive oil

sea salt flakes and freshly ground black pepper

2 broad strips of orange zest

1 bunch of dill, stalks and leaves separated, leaves chopped

⅓ cup freshly squeezed orange juice

for the aïoli

2 garlic cloves, chopped

sea salt flakes

2 medium egg yolks

1 teaspoon Dijon mustard

1 cup fruity extra virgin olive oil, or half extra virgin olive oil and half a more neutral oil

2 tablespoons very finely chopped fennel bulb

Preheat the oven to 400°F.

Rinse the fish in cold water and dry it inside and out with paper towels. Halve the fennel bulbs lengthwise and remove the tough outer leaves from each piece. Remove any leafy fronds and keep them for the aïoli. Trim the bases and cut each half into wedges ¾ inch thick, keeping them intact at the base. Put the wedges into a bowl with the lemon juice, tossing them in it as soon as they're cut, otherwise the flesh will discolor. Add the garlic, half the fennel seeds, ¼ cup of regular olive oil, salt, and pepper. Mix well.

Put the sliced fennel into a roasting pan in which the fish can also fit, tucking the orange zest in among it. Cover with foil and roast the vegetables for 20 minutes. Remove from the oven and toss gently to stop the fennel from sticking to the pan. Fill the cavity of the fish with the dill stalks and half the dill leaves and season generously. Put the sea bass on top of the fennel, sprinkle with regular olive oil and the remaining fennel seeds, and roast for up to 35 minutes, or until the fish flesh is no longer "glassy" and comes away from the bone easily.

Five minutes before the end of the cooking time, pour the orange juice over the vegetables and scatter with the rest of the dill. Transfer the hot fish and vegetables to a warmed serving dish—you need to be careful with the fish as you move it—or let cool a little before moving.

To make the aïoli, crush the garlic with a little salt—the salt acts as an abrasive—scrape into a bowl, and add the egg yolks and mustard. Mix the yolks with the garlic until they are shiny. Beating continuously, either with a wooden spoon or an electric hand mixer, start adding the extra virgin or more neutral oil in tiny drops. Make sure each drop has been incorporated before you add the next. Keep beating and adding oil in a steadily increasing stream.

continued >

fennel fronds (as many as you have retrieved from the fennel above), very finely chopped

½ teaspoon fennel seeds, toasted in a dry skillet and crushed

½ teaspoon Pernod

freshly ground white pepper

juice of up to ½ small lemon (you might not need it all)

If your mixture breaks, just start again with a new egg yolk, and gradually add the curdled mixture to it, going slowly this time. Add the very finely chopped fennel bulb, fennel fronds, and fennel seeds, and finally, the Pernod.

Season with sea salt flakes and white pepper and add the lemon juice little by little, tasting until you're happy.

Serve the fish hot, or slightly cooled, with the aïoli on the side.

tomates provençales aux anchois

I adore anchovies, so have no trouble with the quantities here, but if you are less fond of them—and want a waft rather than a full-on flavor—go for the smaller quantity.

serves 6

8 to 9 large plum tomatoes, halved

1¾- to 3½-oz canned anchovies, in oil, drained (reserve the oil)

2 fat garlic cloves, very finely sliced

sea salt flakes and freshly ground black pepper

1 cup stale coarse white bread crumbs (about 1 day old is good)

finely grated zest of ½ unwaxed lemon

leaves from 4 thyme sprigs

2 tablespoons extra virgin olive oil

Preheat the oven to 375°F.

Put the tomatoes into a gratin dish (you need a big one) in which they can lie in a single layer. They need to be quite snug, but not too squashed up otherwise they sweat; you want some of their moisture to evaporate, as it makes them sweeter.

Halve each anchovy and stick some slices of garlic and some anchovy into each tomato half. Spoon 2 tablespoons of the oil from the anchovies over the tomatoes. Season.

Toss the bread crumbs with the lemon zest, thyme, and seasoning. Scatter the mixture on top of the tomatoes and sprinkle with the extra virgin olive oil. Bake in the oven for 30 to 40 minutes, or until the tomatoes have shrunk and the top is golden brown.

white peaches in chilled moscato

If you don't like Moscato—some people find it cloying—you can use Muscat de Beaumes de Venise or Muscat de Rivesaltes instead. Heavier dessert wines aren't as good; you need something light and floral. If there are diners who don't like dessert wine at all, just give them a perfect peach. I like white peaches—they tend to be more fragrant—but you can also use yellow-fleshed fruits.

serves 6

6 ripe white peaches

1 bottle of Moscato, well chilled

The elegantly simple method for this is described in the introduction to this menu (see page 111). It needs no more explanation.

eating on the cusp

for the slide from summer to autumn

corn cakes with hot-smoked salmon, crème fraîche & salmon caviar

spatchcocked chicken with chile, garlic, parsley & almond *pangrattato*

raspberries, blackberries & figs in late-harvest riesling

It's hard to know whether to feel sad or excited as summer slides into autumn, and it's difficult to pinpoint exactly when summer's gone.

Autumn advances with pincer movements. We teeter between ease and anticipation. It can still be warm and there is an almost embarrassing abundance of fruit and vegetables as the seasons collide. Can I really have figs, late raspberries, *and* corn? I think of America, of all those farm stands where the first pumpkins try to nudge the corn out of the way. Back in my kitchen, I make fruit compotes and American desserts. Those homely fruit-rich slumps and grunts and buckles are perfect at this time of year. They nod to the season to come, as well as to the one that's departing.

And then there's the last of the corn. I'm stupidly romantic about corn. For years, I had a London Transport poster from the 1920s on my bedroom wall. It was called *Flowers o' the Corn* and showed a golden world of poppies and cornflowers growing among corn and grasses. The line at the bottom of the poster read "How Near the Corn Grows." I assume these posters were designed to make you yearn to take a train to the English countryside, but this particular picture made me want to go to the States. I only realized recently that I had always misread the last line, transposing the letters of the first two words. "Now hear the corn grow," I used to whisper when I looked at the image. I daydreamed about lying in a field in the Midwest, cobs of corn towering above me, concentrating on the sound as the corn stalks reached toward the sun. American friends tell me—winking—that you can lie in a cornfield and hear the rustle. As it grows, a corn stalk expands, stretching and crackling. In nature, this happens slowly, but scientists have recorded it and speeded it up. If you want to, you can find recordings online. Hear the corn grow.

This is a goodbye menu, but not a sad one. Goodbye to corn, but hello to smoked food and roasts. If it's warm enough, enjoy summer's last stand in the garden.

corn cakes with hot-smoked salmon, crème fraîche & salmon caviar

I've cooked this dish a million times. It's one of my favorite recipes and comes from the American chef Annie Rosenzweig. She used to make it at her restaurant, Arcadia. When I visited New York for the first time, this was the first dish I ate. She used to serve the cakes with smoked lobster (a little expensive and difficult to get hold of), but you could try smoked scallops or smoked shrimp instead of hot-smoked salmon. Do use fresh ears of corn, though, as canned or frozen corn kernels aren't nearly as good here.

serves 6

for the corn cakes
3 ears of corn, to yield about 2½ cups of kernels

⅓ cup fine cornmeal or polenta

½ cup all-purpose flour

3 large eggs

sea salt flakes and freshly ground black pepper

3 tablespoons unsalted butter, melted and cooled, plus more for frying

peanut oil, for frying

to serve
chopped dill, to serve

10½oz hot-smoked salmon

1 cup crème fraîche

3½oz jar of salmon caviar

lemon wedges

The corn cake batter can be made well in advance. Stand an ear of corn on its end in a roasting pan. Using a sharp knife, cut down the side, removing the kernels from top to bottom. Turn the cob, cutting the corn off in strips all the way around. Repeat for the other 2 ears of corn.

Put all the ingredients (except the butter for frying and the peanut oil) into a food processor and, using the pulse button so as to chop the corn rather than purée it, blitz everything together.

Heat a film of the peanut oil in a skillet and add a bit of butter. Add a couple of tablespoons of the batter to the pan, enough to make a cake 1½ inches across. You can cook about 6 cakes at a time if your skillet is big enough. When each cake has set underneath, flip it over—I use a metal spatula—and cook the other side until golden. Reduce the heat to cook the cakes through. Transfer to a baking pan lined with paper towels and keep the cakes warm in a low oven, in a single layer, while you cook the rest, adding more oil and butter to the skillet as you need it.

Serve the cakes, scattered with dill, with a plateful of hot-smoked salmon (remove the skin and break the salmon into big chunks), a bowlful of crème fraîche, and another of salmon caviar, and lemon wedges.

spatchcocked chicken with chile, garlic, parsley & almond *pangrattato*

I know, this is barely a recipe, it's just flattened roast chicken with chopped almonds and herbs thrown on top, but I really crave this kind of food: charred, juicy meat, a contrasting crunchy texture, and big, strong flavors. It's great for one of those balmy late-summer evening meals.

serves 6

for the chicken
4lb chicken

3 garlic cloves, finely grated

3 tablespoons extra virgin olive oil, divided

sea salt flakes and freshly ground black pepper

8 red onions, cut into wedges

for the pangrattato
⅓ cup extra virgin olive oil

3½oz stale sourdough bread, made into bread crumbs

2 tablespoons chopped blanched almonds

4 garlic cloves, chopped

1 teaspoon crushed red pepper

leaves from a small bunch of flat-leaf parsley, coarsely chopped

finely grated zest of 1 unwaxed lemon

Set the bird on your work surface, breast-side down, legs toward you. Using good kitchen scissors or poultry shears, cut through the flesh and bone along each side of the backbone. Remove the backbone and keep it for stock (freeze it until you've gathered other bones to cook along with it).

Open out the chicken, turn it over so it is skin-side up, then flatten it by pressing hard on the breastbone with the heel of your hand. Remove any big globules of fat and neaten any ragged edges of skin. Now you have a spatchcocked bird.

Gently lift the skin on the breast of the bird so that you can put your hand in between the skin and the flesh (try not to tear the skin). Mix the garlic with 1 tablespoon of the extra virgin olive oil and some seasoning and carefully push this under the skin. Cover with plastic wrap and put in the fridge for a couple of hours.

Preheat the oven to 400°F and take the chicken out of the fridge. Put the onions into a roasting pan and drizzle with the remaining 2 tablespoons of extra virgin olive oil. Set the chicken on top, breast-side up, season the outside, and roast for 1 hour.

Meanwhile, make the *pangrattato*. Heat the extra virgin olive oil in a skillet over medium heat and sauté the bread crumbs in it for about 4 minutes. Add the almonds, garlic, and chile flakes and cook for another minute or so. Remove from the heat and mix with the parsley and lemon zest, chopping everything together.

Cut the chicken into serving pieces and put it onto a warmed platter, on top of the red onions. Pour any extra cooking juices over the top, scatter on the *pangrattato*, and serve.

raspberries, blackberries & figs in late-harvest riesling

I'd rather have some kind of fruit compote than any more complicated dessert, especially in late summer and early autumn when fruit is so abundant. This is perfect to finish a meal at the end of August or beginning of September, when raspberries, blackberries, and figs are all in season at the same time. Serve a simple almond or hazelnut cake on the side, if you like.

serves 6

2 cups late-harvest Riesling, or another medium-weight dessert wine, plus 2 tablespoons

½ cup granulated sugar

12 figs

1 cup mixed blackberries and raspberries

Reserve the 2 tablespoons of the wine. Pour the rest into a broad pan that will hold the halved figs in a single layer and add the sugar. Bring to a boil gently, stirring to help the sugar dissolve, then reduce the heat. Trim the stalks from the figs and halve them lengthwise. Put them in the pan and poach for anywhere from 8 to 14 minutes, depending on their size and ripeness. Watch them carefully; they should be tender but not mushy, and they can become too soft in the blink of an eye.

Lift them out with a slotted spoon as soon as they are ready and put them on a large plate, setting them out separately so that they stop cooking and cool down.

Boil the poaching liquor until you have 1 cup. Let cool, then add the reserved wine. Put the figs in a bowl with the blackberries and pour over the syrup, but don't add the raspberries until about 15 minutes before serving, as they become too soft if left steeping. I like this chilled, but serve it at room temperature if you prefer.

autumn and winter

a thousand chiles

mexican warmth

ceviche de sierra

tinga poblana | *arroz verde* | roast pumpkin & cauliflower with black beans & cascabel chiles

mango cheeks in lime & ginger syrup

The Aeromexico plane is being buffeted as if it was a toy, the windows illuminated every so often by lightning. "*Padre nuestro que está en los cielos*," the woman behind me prays in whispers. I feel guilty that my dominant emotion is exhilaration. Thirty minutes later I'm running across the tarmac, as my clothes get drenched by dark rain. My carry-on luggage—a cardboard box that houses a gaudy *papier-mâché* candelabra in the shape of a tree, tendrils of mad flowers clutching its trunk, wise owls sitting on its branches (bought because it reflected what I saw around me, vivid colors, a crazy kind of magic, and a quiet sagacity in the people)—is so wet it's falling apart. At 1 A.M. I swing through the doors of my hotel in Mérida to find a band playing "La Bamba," and a bar serving *antojitos* (little snacks) of shrimp fritters, chile peanuts, and pickled fava beans. There's a mezcal menu taped to the wall. I'm suddenly so happy it's as if I'd drunk my way through the list. Mexico, I think…it's a hip-swinging, toe-tapping head rush.

This was my first trip to the country, defiantly undertaken after being dumped by my boyfriend. It's a good place to mend a broken heart. I knew nothing about Mexican cooking—though I expected guacamole—and wasn't prepared for the extremes or the intricacies of the food. Some plates were citrus-fresh and simple: there was ceviche, slivers of pearlescent fish, their edges opaque from being "cooked" in lime juice, served with raw onion, chile, and avocado. Other dishes were deep and layered: moles, the sauces for which Mexico is famous, slow braises, meat cooked in pits. You could see the colors—and the emotions—of Mexico's most famous painters, Diego Rivera and Frida Kahlo, in the food on your table.

When I got to Oaxaca, a beautiful city three hundred miles from the capital, I wanted my own kitchen, there was just so much to experiment with. The market sold fruits I'd never seen, a drink made from fermented pineapple, thousands of leathery chiles, and baskets of spiced dried grasshoppers. In the middle of it all there was a vendor clutching a bunch of iridescent balloons. They shimmered. I wondered if this was what was meant by magical realism. If the balloon vendor had started to float heavenward I wouldn't have been surprised. I forgot all about the boyfriend.

To me, the great complex cuisines had been French and Chinese, but now I came to think that you couldn't call yourself a cook if you hadn't mastered Mexican sauces, their flavors built slowly and gradually. The dried chiles weren't about heat, but tone. They have a certain masculinity—they make you think of wood, tobacco, ripe autumnal fruit, chocolate—and provide the cook with a vast array of notes. I came to crave the sweet vanilla aroma of corn, the scent I most associate with Mexico. For years after this trip, every time I drank a cold beer I would simultaneously smell the blistered cobs sold on street carts and the corn boiled with lime and ground to make *masa harina* (the body and soul of tortillas).

Mexicans are modest, and they've never shouted about their food, but high-profile Mexican chefs are now demolishing the idea that their country's cuisine is merely avocados and tortilla chips. It's also about crimson hibiscus flowers, Mexican oregano, roses, cinnamon, and allspice. And corn and beer, lime and tomatillos, and the smoky chipotles that fixed my heart that summer.

ceviche de sierra

Ceviche—raw fish and citrus juice—always surprises me. There is no cooking, other than the "cooking" that is the result of lime juice on fish flesh—yet it's so rich and satisfying. Use whichever fish you fancy; mackerel is probably the best-value option. And make sure it is *absolutely* fresh.

serves 6

4 spanking-fresh fillets, 1lb in total, of mackerel, porgy, sea bass (branzino), fluke, or red snapper, skinned

juice of 3 limes, divided

1 shallot, very finely sliced

1 large ripe avocado, or 2 smaller avocados

sea salt flakes and freshly ground black pepper

1 red and 1 green chile, halved, seeded, and finely sliced

¼ cup avocado oil or extra virgin olive oil

⅓ cup cilantro leaves, coarsely chopped

¼ cup pomegranate seeds

Slice the fish fillets on the diagonal into broad strips, similar to the way you would slice smoked salmon. Put them into a dish with the juice of 2 of the limes and the shallot.

Halve the avocado (or avocados), remove the stone(s), and cut the flesh into slices. Peel the skin from each slice, put these into a broad, shallow serving bowl or onto a platter, season, then squeeze the juice of the remaining lime over them.

Add the chiles, the fish, and shallot, the avocado or extra virgin olive oil, and the cilantro. Sprinkle with the pomegranate seeds and serve.

tinga poblana

This recipe is often made with chicken, but I prefer a richer, slower-cooked pork version. The roasting of the tomatoes is very important here: you need scorched flesh and a slight caramelization.

serves 6

4 dried chipotle chiles

3lb plum tomatoes, halved

regular olive oil

sea salt flakes and freshly ground black pepper

2 teaspoons soft light brown sugar

8oz chorizo (the type that needs to be cooked)

peanut oil (optional)

3lb boneless pork shoulder, cut into 1½-inch cubes

2 onions, coarsely chopped

4 garlic cloves, crushed

2 teaspoons ground cumin

4 thyme sprigs

2 teaspoons dried oregano (preferably Mexican)

about 1 cup chicken stock or water

to serve

2 ripe avocados

juice of 1 lime

1 scant cup sour cream

3 tablespoons coarsely chopped cilantro

5½oz mild, chalky goat cheese (don't use a soft and creamy cheese here), or feta or Lancashire cheese, crumbled

Preheat the oven to 375°F. Cover the chipotles with just-boiled water (only enough to cover) and let soak.

Put the tomatoes, cut-side up, into a roasting pan where they can lie in a single layer. Drizzle with olive oil, season, and sprinkle with sugar. Roast for 45 to 50 minutes, until shrunken and scorched in patches.

Peel the casing off of the chorizo and chop the meat. Heat 1 tablespoon peanut oil (or regular olive oil) in a large skillet and sauté the chorizo until well colored all over. Transfer it to a Dutch oven, retaining its fat in the skillet. Brown the pork in batches in this fat over medium-high heat (if the pan is crowded it will just sweat). Get a really good color all over. Transfer each batch to the Dutch oven.

You will probably have enough oil left in the skillet for the onions but, if not, add a little more. Fry the onions until they are a good dark gold. Add the garlic and cumin and cook for 2 minutes more, then add all this to the Dutch oven with the thyme, oregano, and seasoning. Deglaze the pan with some of the stock or water (unless anything burned in it) and add this to the Dutch oven with the rest of the stock.

Remove the chipotles from their liquid (keep the liquid), take off and discard the stalks, remove the seeds (leave some of them in if you want a little more heat), and chop the flesh. Add these, with their soaking liquid, to the Dutch oven. Bring to a boil, then reduce the heat to low and cook gently, partially covered, for 90 minutes. Halfway through the cooking time, coarsely chop the tomatoes and add them, and all their cooking juices, to the meat. By the end of the cooking time the pork should be tender and the *tinga* nice and thick.

To serve, halve, pit, and slice the avocados, then peel the skin off of each slice. Squeeze lime juice all over them and season. Put the meat into a large, warmed, broad bowl (or serve from the Dutch oven in which it has cooked) and spoon over some sour cream (serve the rest on the side). Scatter with cilantro. Offer the cheese at the table.

arroz verde

This is served on special occasions—festivals and weddings—in Mexico. Plain boiled rice would be fine with the pork instead, if you want to keep things simpler.

serves 6

2 garlic cloves, chopped

1 green chile, halved, seeded, and chopped

2 scallions, chopped

1 cup spinach leaves

⅓ cup parsley leaves

¾ cup cilantro leaves

2¼ cups long-grain rice

1½ tablespoons peanut oil

1 onion, very finely chopped

2½ cups chicken stock

a little unsalted butter

finely grated zest and juice of 1 lime

sea salt flakes and freshly ground black pepper

Put the garlic, chile, scallions, spinach, and herbs into a blender along with ½ cup of water and whiz to a purée. You might need to scrape down the sides of the blender and whiz again to make sure it has all puréed properly.

Wash the rice in water, then rinse it in a sieve until the water runs clear. Heat half the oil in a large saucepan and sauté the onion until it's soft but not colored. Add the rice and turn it over in the oil, cooking it for a couple of minutes. Add the stock and bring to a boil.

Boil the rice until the surface of the rice is "pitted" with little holes (small air holes appear on the surface of the rice). Meanwhile, heat the rest of the oil in a skillet and sauté the green purée until it no longer smells "raw" (it takes a matter of minutes; the smell of raw garlic should have gone). Add this to the rice, trying not to fork it through too much.

Cover the pan and cook over very low heat for another 5 minutes, then take the pan off the heat, cover the surface with well-buttered parchment paper, and put the lid back on. Let the rice cook in its own steam for another 15 minutes or so. The grains should be tender.

Add the lime zest and juice and mix it thoroughly using a fork. Check the seasoning before serving.

roast pumpkin & cauliflower with black beans & cascabel chiles

serves 6

6 cascabel chiles

5 garlic cloves, finely chopped, divided

⅔ cup peanut oil

2¼lb pumpkin flesh, peeled and cut into chunks

1 medium cauliflower, in florets

2 onions, cut into wedges

1 to 2 teaspoons crushed red pepper

1 tablespoon regular olive oil

15oz can of black beans, rinsed

juice of 1 lime

finely grated zest of 3 limes

¼ cup cilantro leaves

Preheat the oven to 375°F. Toast the chiles in a dry skillet, turning them over until the color changes (it only takes a couple of minutes). Put them in a bowl and cover with just-boiled water. Let soak for 20 minutes, then drain. Remove the stalks. Blend the chiles with 3 of the garlic cloves and the peanut oil, whizzing to a purée.

Divide the vegetables between 2 roasting pans, season with salt and pepper, and toss with the cascabel purée and the chile flakes. Roast for 30 minutes, turning the vegetables over every so often.

Heat the regular olive oil in a medium skillet, heat the beans through in this, and season. Transfer the vegetables to a serving dish and gently mix in the beans. Squeeze the lime juice on top. Chop the zest, cilantro, and the remaining 2 garlic cloves together and scatter them over the vegetables—this just lifts the dish—then serve.

mango cheeks in lime & ginger syrup

Mangoes arranged like this, the fruit sliced but still in the shape of the "cheeks" that lie on each side of the stone, were included in one of Antonio Carluccio's early books, also with a syrup. I thought it looked beautiful and have been serving it this way for years. Slices of fresh pineapple and wheels of pink and white grapefruit are also lovely in the same syrup. Fruit and lime are exactly what you need at the end of this meal.

serves 6

6 limes

¾ cup granulated sugar

1¼-inch piece fresh ginger root, peeled and finely sliced

3 medium, perfectly ripe mangoes, peeled

Remove the zest from 2 of the limes with a zester. Put this in a bowl, cover, and reserve. Finely grate the zest of another 2 limes and put it into a saucepan. Juice all 6 of the limes and add the juice to the saucepan, with 1½ cups of water, the sugar, and ginger root. Heat gently, stirring from time to time to help the sugar dissolve. Bring to a boil, then reduce the heat and simmer for 7 to 10 minutes, or until it is very slightly syrupy looking (it becomes more syrupy as it cools). Cool, then chill.

Cut off the "cheeks" from the mangoes; you do this by cutting through the flesh, alongside the central seed, so you are left with 2 rounded, fleshy sides and a seed that still has quite a lot of fruit around it. You are only going to use the cheeks for this dish, so keep the rest of the flesh for something else (or just eat it).

Lay the cheeks on a chopping board and cut each into slices, holding onto the mango flesh so the slices stay together in their cheek shape. Carefully place each sliced cheek in a broad shallow bowl. Add the reserved lime zest to the chilled syrup and pour this over the slices.

smoky days

lunch for early autumn

apple in the mist

crab cakes with cucumber pickle

cheddar, onion & spinach tart

cider & apple jellies with rosemary & cider brandy syllabub

It's never easy to say when the change takes place. The smoky afternoons can arrive gradually or suddenly, usually around the third week of September. You begin to notice that it isn't just the light that's different at 4 p.m., but the texture of the air, too. It becomes gauzy. It smells different as well; there's a sweet woodiness, and a dampness. You want to make soup and tarts, and start to crave apples and pears. It's a phase that's worth marking with a meal.

apple in the mist

I don't often make up cocktail recipes, but I wanted to come up with something that tasted of autumn and baked apples. I like this so much it's now my cold weather tipple. If you want it more apple-y (and less alcoholic) add 2 to 3 tablespoons of sweet apple cider (a more tart one, made from a specific variety, if you can).

makes 1

thin slices of tawny-skinned apple

juice of 1 lemon, divided

3 tablespoons English cider brandy or French calvados

2 tablespoons bourbon

1 teaspoon maple syrup
dash of Angostura bitters

Put the slices of apple—they look best if they are cut horizontally, so that you can see the star shape in the middle of each slice—into half the lemon juice to stop them discoloring.

Pour everything else, including the remaining lemon juice, into a cocktail shaker with ice. Shake and pour. Add an apple slice to each drink.

crab cakes with cucumber pickle

These truly are crab cakes—no potato, no "filler" other than enough bread crumbs to help the crab meat to bind together—and they're pretty rich, so just two small cakes for each person is fine.

serves 6

for the cucumber pickle

2 cucumbers

1½ onions

2 small green bell peppers, halved and seeded

2 tablespoons sea salt flakes

2 cups white wine vinegar

2 cups superfine sugar

generous pinch of saffron threads

1 tablespoon celery seeds

1 tablespoon dill seeds

2½ tablespoons wholegrain mustard

for the crab cakes

13oz fresh lump crab meat

1½ cups white bread crumbs

2½ tablespoons finely chopped flat-leaf parsley leaves

1 teaspoon English mustard

good pinch of cayenne pepper

sea salt flakes and freshly ground black pepper

2 medium eggs, lightly beaten

all-purpose flour, to coat

sunflower, peanut, or vegetable oil, for frying

lemon wedges, to serve

watercress, to serve

Make the cucumber pickle first, as it needs to cool. It keeps for ages, so you can make it well in advance (I've got a jar in my fridge that's been there for more than a year).

Slice the cucumbers very finely, along with the onions and green bell peppers. Mix the vegetables with the salt and put in a colander set over a bowl. Let stand for 2 hours.

Bring the remaining ingredients—except the mustard—to a boil in a saucepan. Drain the vegetables, rinse and pat them dry, and add them to the vinegar mixture. Return to a boil, then stir in the mustard. Put into a sterilized jar with a vinegar-proof lid (see page 86) and seal.

Mix together the crab, bread crumbs, parsley, mustard, cayenne, and seasoning and add the eggs gradually, until you have a mixture firm enough to mold with your hands.

Put some flour on a plate. Form 12 crab cakes, each about 2½ inches across, and dip each side in the flour. Transfer to a baking sheet as they're made. Cover with plastic wrap and put them in the fridge to chill for 1 hour (this is crucial, or they'll just fall apart).

Heat a thin film of your chosen oil in a skillet and cook the cakes over medium-high heat for 4 minutes on each side, reducing the heat once the cakes have a good color on the outside. They should be golden, crispy, and cooked through.

Serve 2 crab cakes per person with lemon wedges, watercress, and the cucumber pickle. I also like to serve a bowl of crème fraîche into which I've stirred a little finely grated garlic and chopped soft herbs such as chives and parsley, so add that as well if you like.

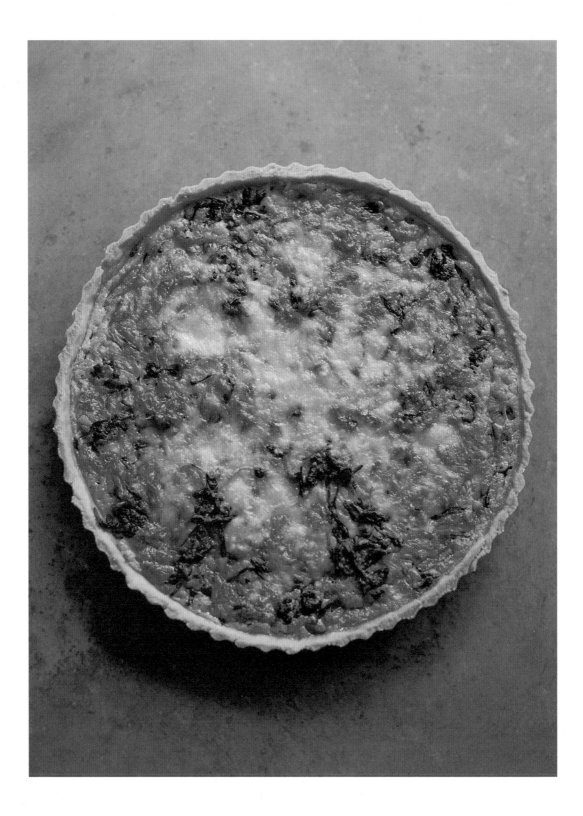

cheddar, onion & spinach tart

I adore tarts (melting pastry and a soft filling are so comforting) and cheesy tarts in particular. This dish feels very British. I usually serve it with hard cider.

serves 6

for the pastry

2¼ cups all-purpose flour, plus more to dust

1¼ sticks chilled unsalted butter, chopped

sea salt flakes

2 large egg yolks

for the filling

2 tablespoons unsalted butter

1¼lb onions, very finely sliced

6 garlic cloves, finely sliced

1lb spinach, coarse stalks removed

freshly ground black pepper

2 large eggs, plus 3 egg yolks

1½ cups heavy cream

2 teaspoons English mustard

5½oz extra-sharp Cheddar cheese, grated

For the pastry, put the flour, butter, and a good pinch of salt into a food processor and whiz until it resembles bread crumbs. Add the yolks and a little ice-cold water (about 2 teaspoons), and whiz to bring it into a ball. Shape into a disk, seal in plastic wrap, and chill for 30 minutes.

Melt the butter for the filling in a large heavy saucepan and cook the onions and garlic, with a little salt, until slightly golden, then add a good splash of water and cover. Let sweat over very low heat until the onions are soft and floppy, about 30 minutes, stirring every so often.

Preheat the oven to 350°F. Place a baking pan in it. Roll out the pastry on a lightly floured surface and use it to line a loose-bottomed tart pan, 11 inches in diameter (keep any leftover pastry). Chill for 30 minutes in the cold part of the fridge, or the freezer.

Uncover the onions, increase the heat, and let the excess moisture bubble off and the onions cook until they are golden and sweet.

Wash the spinach and cook in a covered pan with just the water left clinging to it, for about 4 minutes over medium heat, until wilted, turning over the mass every so often to make sure all of it is in contact with the bottom of the pan. Drain in a colander and let cool.

Line the pastry crust with nonstick parchment paper, fill with pie weights, and bake blind on the hot baking pan for 15 minutes. Remove the paper and weights and cook for another 8 minutes. Take it out of the oven and use the leftover raw pastry to patch any cracks you see.

Squeeze excess moisture from the spinach (with your fists or between 2 dinner plates) chop, season, and add to the onions. Mix the eggs, yolks, cream, and mustard and season well. Spread the spinach mixture into the crust, sprinkle with the cheese, and pour on the cream mixture. Place on the hot baking pan in the oven and bake for 30 minutes, until just a little soft in the middle and golden. It will continue to cook once out of the oven. Let cool for 10 to 15 minutes, then serve. A salad of bitter greens is good on the side.

cider & apple jellies with rosemary & cider brandy syllabub

There are quite a few elements here—a gelatin layer, stewed fruit, syllabub—but each is simple and gives you the flavor of apples in a different form and texture. If you don't have English cider brandy, then use Calvados. And in the absence of either, brandy or whiskey will do. In the UK I use cold-pressed apple juice for this, though it can be difficult to find. If you don't use that the jellies will be cloudy, but it doesn't make any difference to the flavor. Jellies made from scratch—with gelatin and fruit juice or sweetened alcohol—are one of the glories of British cookery. And they're easy to make once you get the hang of them.

serves 6

for the syllabub
1 rosemary sprig

3 tablespoons granulated sugar, or to taste

juice of ½ small lemon

3 tablespoons Somerset cider brandy, apple brandy, or Calvados, or to taste

1 tablespoon apple juice

¾ cup heavy cream

for the cider gelatin layer
½oz gelatin leaves (they can be any grade, though I use platinum as it gives a clearer jelly)

1½ cups hard dry cider

3½ cups cider

¼ cup granulated sugar

2 broad strips of unwaxed lemon zest

1 tablespoon Somerset cider brandy, apple brandy, or Calvados

for the apple layer
1lb 5oz cooking apples

3 tablespoons superfine sugar

Start the syllabub the day before you want to serve the dessert; you just need to do this first step. Put the rosemary and sugar into a mortar and bash it with the pestle. As the sugar breaks down, the rosemary will perfume it. Transfer to a small saucepan and add the lemon juice, brandy, and apple juice. Heat gently until the sugar dissolves, but don't let it boil. Remove it from the heat and let infuse overnight.

For the jelly, put the gelatin in a bowl and cover with cold water. Let soak for 5 minutes. Put the hard cider, apple juice, sugar, and zest into a saucepan and gradually heat, stirring to help the sugar dissolve. Let this cool until it is still warm, but you can put your hand in it. Remove the zest. Lift the gelatin out of its water—it should be completely soft—and squeeze out the excess. Add to the hard cider mixture and stir until melted (you can't add gelatin to very hot liquid as it impairs the setting qualities, but it does have to completely dissolve). Add the brandy. Divide among 6 glasses (they need to be big enough to take the other components as well) and put in the fridge to set.

Peel and core the apples and coarsely slice. Put into a pan with about 2 tablespoons water and the superfine sugar. Let it stew over medium heat until completely soft, then mash to a purée (finer than regular "stewed" apples, but not as smooth as baby food). Let cool completely.

Quite close to serving time, as the elements of syllabub can separate if they sit for too long, strain the infused rosemary liquid you made the day before into a bowl. Add the cream and beat gradually until it thickens into soft folds. I do this with an electric hand mixer so I can keep a good eye on it. It can get thick very suddenly, so watch it.

Taste and add more sugar or brandy as needed. Assemble the dessert by putting a layer of apples on top of each cider gelatin layer, then topping off with generous and luxurious folds of the syllabub.

i can never resist pumpkins

soup and simplicity

autumn vegetables with hazelnut, roast bell pepper & anchovy relish

pumpkin soup with sage butter

tuscan grape bread & italian cheeses

biccerin

Pumpkins are ubiquitous now, but there were none to be found in Northern Ireland when I was growing up. Even when I moved to London in the mid-1980s they were hard to get hold of. I read about them in the *Little House on the Prairie* books when I was a child and I longed for them. I think that's why I still see them as some kind of enchanted ingredient. I love their different shapes and colors, their sweet flavor, and their yielding, velvety flesh. Over the years I've cooked them every which way and often, as here, build an entire autumnal meal around them.

autumn vegetables with hazelnut, roast bell pepper & anchovy relish

I make a lot of different nut relishes. They have such a varied texture—part puréed, part coarse—and work so well with both sweet and bitter vegetables. This relish is also good with meaty fish or with lamb.

serves 6 to 8

for the relish
1 fat garlic clove, coarsely chopped

¼ teaspoon sea salt flakes

1 cup toasted hazelnuts

2oz can of really good-quality anchovies, drained and chopped

⅓ cup extra virgin olive oil

1 teaspoon white balsamic vinegar

¼ cup finely chopped flat-leaf parsley leaves

3 red bell peppers

for the vegetables
14oz fat Jerusalem artichokes, scrubbed

regular olive oil

16 stalks of broccolini

leaves from 2 heads of red Belgian endive

1 bunch of French breakfast radishes, halved if you like (with the leaves, if really fresh)

Preheat the oven to 375°F.

Grind the garlic and salt to a paste in a mortar. Add the nuts and anchovies and pound until you have a mixture that is partly puréed, partly chunky.

Stir in the extra virgin olive oil, white balsamic vinegar, some freshly ground black pepper, and the parsley. Set aside.

Halve the Jerusalem artichokes lengthwise and steam for about 10 minutes. Pat dry, place in a roasting pan, and brush with regular olive oil. Halve and seed the bell peppers and put into another roasting pan. Brush them, too, with regular olive oil. Roast both pans of vegetables for 25 to 30 minutes, or until the vegetables are completely tender.

When the bell peppers are cool enough to handle, slip off and discard their skins, chop the flesh, and add it to the hazelnut relish. It should be a little sloppy, so you might want to add a bit more extra virgin olive oil. Check for seasoning.

Lightly cook the broccolini (steam or boil it for 3 to 4 minutes) then put it on a platter with the Jerusalem artichokes, Belgian endive leaves, and radishes, along with any radish leaves. Serve with the relish.

pumpkin soup with sage butter

Get a good pumpkin for this, with the sweetest flesh you can find. If you're not going to follow the soup with the cheese and bread (as suggested on pages 156–7), shavings of Parmesan cheese are good on top.

serves 6 to 8

3lb 5oz pumpkin, peeled, seeded, and flesh cut into large chunks

3 tablespoons regular olive oil

sea salt flakes and freshly ground black pepper

1 stick unsalted butter

2 leeks, washed, trimmed, and sliced into disks

½ onion, coarsely chopped

6 cups chicken stock

24 sage leaves

Preheat the oven to 375°F.

Put the pumpkin flesh in a roasting pan. Toss it in the regular olive oil and season. Put the pan in the oven and cook for 15 to 20 minutes, or until the flesh is completely tender and golden.

Meanwhile, melt half the butter in a heavy, broad saucepan and add the leeks and onion. Season. Cover the pan and sweat the leeks and onion over low heat for about 20 minutes, adding a splash of water every so often to stop the mixture from sticking and burning.

Add the pumpkin to the leeks and onion. Pour in the stock, season, and bring to a boil. Reduce the heat and simmer for 15 minutes, then purée in batches in a blender and check the seasoning.

To serve, melt the remaining butter in a skillet and, over medium heat, sauté the sage leaves for about 1 minute until slightly crisp.

Top each warmed bowl of soup with 3 to 4 sage leaves and a drizzle of the melted butter they were cooked in.

tuscan grape bread & italian cheeses

This is a joy to make and to serve; the bread becomes blotchy with the purple juice of the grapes as it bakes. Pure autumn.

serves 8

2 teaspoons active dry yeast

2 tablespoons superfine sugar

1¼ cups lukewarm water

4 cups white bread flour, plus more to dust

1 teaspoon sea salt flakes

¼ cup extra virgin olive oil, plus more to handle the dough

semolina, to dust

¼ cup dark raisins

½ cup Marsala

1lb 2oz seedless red grapes

about 8 rosemary or thyme sprigs

1 tablespoon soft light brown sugar

Taleggio, Gorgonzola, or Fontina, and other strong Italian cheeses, to serve

Put the yeast into a small bowl with 1 teaspoon of the superfine sugar and a couple of tablespoons of the water. Stir, then let stand somewhere warm to froth for 15 minutes or so.

Put the flour into a bowl with the salt and the remaining superfine sugar and make a well in the middle. Pour the yeast mixture into this and start to mix in the surrounding flour. (I usually begin with a butter knife, but you can use your hands right from the start.) Gradually add the rest of the water, or as much as you need to make a soft, rather wet dough. When it has come together, knead it for 10 minutes. Put into a lightly oiled bowl, turn to coat the dough with a film of oil, then cover the bowl with plastic wrap. Let stand somewhere warm to rise for a couple of hours. It should double in size.

Now you need to punch down the dough by kneading it a little on a lightly floured surface. Shape into a disk measuring about 9 inches across. Put on a baking pan dusted with semolina and let proof for 30 minutes. Preheat the oven to 350°F.

Put the raisins and Marsala in a small saucepan and bring to a boil, then take the pan off the heat, and leave the raisins to plump up. They should absorb all the liquid.

Press the whole grapes into the dough and scatter with the rosemary or thyme (use a mixture of leaves and stems with leaves still attached). Sprinkle with the brown sugar and drizzle with the ¼ cup of extra virgin olive oil. Put it in the oven and bake for 45 minutes, or until the bread is cooked (if you lever it off the baking pan and tap it underneath, it should sound slightly hollow). When there are just 10 minutes left before the end of cooking time, spoon the raisins evenly over the top of the bread, too.

Let the loaf cool slightly and serve warm, or at room temperature, with the cheese.

biccerin

A specialty of Turin in Piedmont (chocolate is a big thing there), and a great drink for autumn and winter. I have been known to add booze (grappa or brandy). You must imagine yourself in a mirrored Torinese café—under crystal chandeliers—as you drink it.

makes 6 to 8

1½ cups heavy cream

confectioners' sugar, to taste

3¼ cups whole milk

10½oz dark chocolate, 70 percent cocoa solids, chopped

3 tablespoons granulated sugar

2 cups hot, very strong coffee or espresso

Whip the cream until it holds its shape, then sweeten it to taste with confectioners' sugar.

Heat the milk in a large saucepan with the chocolate and granulated sugar. Whisk until it begins to boil, then reduce the heat and let it simmer for 1 minute, whisking all the time.

Pour the coffee into 6 to 8 heatproof glasses. Carefully and slowly pour the chocolate mixture on top. Top off with the whipped cream and serve.

october is the best month

it's my birthday and i'll eat what i want to

scallops with bitter greens, brown butter & fresh horseradish

slow-roast duck legs with sweet-sour plums

pear, blackberry & hazelnut cake

October is my favorite month. I even like the shape of the word on the page. The "O," because it's closed, suggests you'll be held, and indeed it's the "settling down" month, the month when you turn back toward home. August allows—even demands—a lack of structure, odd meal times, even no meals at all (you might prefer just to down an icy draft of juice, then press the cold glass against your cheek). September is a month of beginnings: new shoes, empty exercise books, possibilities. In October, even before anyone has lit a bonfire, you smell smoke in the air and you want to taste it, too; I poach smoked haddock in milk and wonder if it's extravagant to buy a whole smoked duck. Gradually it gets colder. You put a sweater on and realize that the world has shifted and you've returned to the kitchen. Of course I'm there in the summer, too, but only for brief stints, long enough to make a tomato salad or griddle chicken. Now, I take hold of it again and it feels like returning to someone you love. It might be because I was born in October—or maybe because I'm a bit of a hibernator—but I recognize the world at this time of year, I know its food, I like its smells and rhythms; October is where I'm from.

In Northern Ireland, where I grew up, October is the best month. Blackberries ripen later there, so we always went picking at the end of September and the beginning of October. We would come home, carrying colanders of the black fruits, just as it was starting to get dark and shreds of mist were settling over the fields. We'd make a crisp before the fruit started to spoil; someone would be dispatched to the gas station down the road (hub of gossip and emporium of everything you could possibly need) for vanilla ice cream and so the evening kicked off with dessert. By the end of the month, the trees' skeletons, stripped of their leaves, had appeared, and in the mornings they were white with frost. I loved the cold air filling my lungs as I walked past them on glittering pavement on my way to school.

I start baking in October just because I want to be in the kitchen, sifting and weighing and doing things slowly. Bread dough rises, hands are covered in flour, your apron is never off. It isn't just dishes that change with the seasons, it's how you cook, how you want to move round the kitchen. Come autumn, I cook as if on autopilot, as if my body remembers what to do. When I brown meat for a braise—turning it over and adjusting the heat so that it gets just the right amount of caramelization—I barely think about it. Later in the process, I know when—and by how much—to move the lid on the casserole, nudging it so that the stock around the meat can reduce. This is different from spring and summer cooking, when you have to be nimble, turning fillets of salmon over just at the moment the skin is golden and crispy but not scorched. Autumn cooking is not about instant flavors or assemblies of startling contrasts; it's about layering and waiting.

Then, of course, there's October's food: sweet pumpkins, milky hazelnuts, drowsy looking pears, plump mussels in their inky shells. You can re-embrace dried foods too. I no longer stand holding a bag of lentils thinking it's too warm to cook them; instead they're turned into Middle Eastern purées or Indian dals, or tossed in mustardy dressings.

October also brings Halloween. In Great Britain some decry it as an American import, but it's actually an Irish festival (19th-century Irish immigrants took it to the States). The best party I ever gave was as an 11-year-old one Halloween. We weren't allowed fireworks in Northern Ireland because of the Troubles, and there you carve lanterns from turnips (no easy task) not pumpkins (the turnip smelt bitter as its flesh became singed inside). My dad lit a bonfire and we put out platters of fat sausage rolls and sticky pork ribs on the dining room table. Kenny, our family butcher, came with his guitar and sang Johnny Cash and Burl Ives songs (he thought "Big Rock Candy Mountain" was good, because it was a tease, but we all preferred "Ring of Fire"), as we sat on the floor eating apple and blackberry crisp.

This is such a good party, I thought, a party of bonfires and smoke and fruit and lanterns and warmth.

It could only have happened in October.

scallops with bitter greens, brown butter & fresh horseradish

If scallops are on a menu, I will always order them. They're less briny than crab, less sweet than lobster, the flavor perfectly poised between the two. I love the shape as well: a puck of creamy meat with a comma-shaped coral attached. Their sweetness contrasts well here with the heat of horseradish and the bitterness of Belgian endive. If you can find *radicchio di Treviso*—it looks like crimson feathers—then use it; the leaves are beautiful.

serves 8

24 fat sea scallops, cleaned

2 small heads of red Belgian endive or *radicchio di Treviso*

1 small head of white Belgian endive

1½ tablespoons white balsamic vinegar

4½ tablespoons extra virgin olive oil

sea salt flakes and freshly ground black pepper

regular olive oil

juice of 1 lemon

2¾oz fresh horseradish (peeled weight), coarsely grated

1 stick unsalted butter

Allow the scallops to come to room temperature. Check each to see whether there is a little white bit at the edge: this gets tough during cooking, so slice it off if it's there. Pat the scallops dry with paper towels; if they're wet they won't brown well.

Trim the base of each head of Belgian endive or *radicchio di Treviso* and separate the leaves. Toss them in a bowl with the white balsamic vinegar and extra virgin olive oil and season. Divide the leaves among 8 plates.

Now you need to work quickly. Heat 2 large skillets until they're very hot. Brush the scallops on both sides with some of the regular olive oil. Add the scallops to the skillets and cook for 1 minute on each side, seasoning with salt and pepper, though they may need a further 30 seconds if they're really big. Don't crowd the pan or the scallops will just sweat, and keep the heat high; you want the seared surfaces to be dotted with gold and the centers to have just lost any pearly translucence. Add a good squeeze of lemon juice to each pan (you don't have to use the juice of the entire lemon).

Divide the scallops among the plates. Scatter the horseradish on top.

For this final stage it would be a good idea to enlist help a few minutes before serving as, ideally, the brown butter should be ready at the same time as the scallops. In a small saucepan, melt the butter over medium heat and cook until it begins to brown and smell nutty (about 3 minutes, but be careful not to burn it). Take off the heat and drizzle it over each serving. Serve immediately.

slow-roast duck legs with sweet-sour plums

This recipe gives you slightly more plums than you need, but cooking fewer doesn't work very well (the small amount of juice the fruit produces simply evaporates). Just make the quantity here and keep the leftovers in the fridge; their sweet-sour fruitiness is perfect with cold meats, terrines and pâtés, and pork chops. I've kept them for a good six months in the past. Once you've made the plums, all you have to do on the day is roast the duck legs—there isn't even any carving—and make a side dish. Green salad with hazelnut oil dressing (see page 187) is good, as well as something starchy.

serves 8

for the plums

2¾lb plums, preferably with crimson flesh

1 scant cup white wine vinegar or apple cider vinegar

1 scant cup red wine

2½ cups granulated sugar or 2 cups firmly packed soft light brown sugar, or to taste

½ tablespoon coriander seeds, crushed

½ tablespoon yellow mustard seeds

1 cinnamon stick, broken in half

½ teaspoon ground mace

seeds from 8 cardamom pods, ground

2 red chiles, halved, seeded, and finely sliced

for the duck

10 rosemary sprigs

10 garlic cloves

8 duck legs

sea salt flakes and freshly ground black pepper

Preheat the oven to 325°F.

Halve and pit the plums and put them in a roasting pan with all the other plum ingredients. The plums have to be able to lie in a single layer. Bake for about 45 minutes. Now have a look and taste. You may need to adjust the sugar, depending on how tart the fruit is. Put the pan back into the oven and cook until the mixture is glossy and the chunks of soft plum are surrounded by a rich, thick syrup; this can take anything from 1½ to 2½ hours, depending on how ripe and juicy the plums are, and you'll need to check every so often to see how they are doing and to stir them gently. Remember that syrups thicken as they cool. If you find that the plums are very dark, but you still have too much liquid, drain it off and reduce it by boiling, then return it to the plums. Let cool, then keep in the fridge, but return to room temperature before serving.

When you're ready to cook the duck, preheat the oven to 350°F. Lay the rosemary sprigs and garlic cloves in a roasting pan in which the duck legs can lie in a single layer (you may need 2 pans) and arrange the duck on top. Sprinkle with salt and pepper and roast for 1 hour, then check to see whether the duck is cooked through. (Strain off the duck fat and keep it for roasting potatoes another day.)

Serve the duck with the plums and some mashed potatoes, mashed celery root, potatoes sautéed in duck fat, or even a barley pilaf.

pear, blackberry & hazelnut cake

The duck main course—indeed, any duck dish—needs something uncomplicated to follow it. A simple loaf cake such as this is a good thing and doesn't have to be kept just for teatime. This recipe contains three of my favorite autumn ingredients—pears, blackberries, and hazelnuts—and the blackberries give lovely bursts of sharpness; I like to serve more on the side. A mulled red wine sorbet would also be lovely at the end of this meal, if you don't want to bake a cake, or try a simple apple tart.

serves 8

unsalted butter, for the pan

1⅔ cups all-purpose flour, divided

1 large pear, peeled, cored, and chopped

1 cup blackberries, plus more to serve

2 teaspoons baking powder

1 cup packed soft light brown sugar

pinch of sea salt flakes

1 cup plain full-fat yogurt

½ cup regular olive oil

3 large eggs, at room temperature, lightly beaten

1 teaspoon vanilla extract

finely grated zest of ½ orange

⅓ cup hazelnuts, toasted and very coarsely chopped

confectioners' sugar, to dust

Preheat the oven to 350°F and butter a loaf pan measuring 9½ x 5 x 2½ inches. Line the bottom with nonstick parchment paper.

Toss 2 big spoonfuls of the flour with the pear and blackberries. Put the rest of the flour in a large bowl and add the baking powder, sugar, and salt.

Mix together the yogurt with the regular olive oil in a cup and add the eggs, vanilla, and orange zest.

Stir the wet ingredients into the flour mixture, making sure the flour is properly mixed in, carefully fold in the floured fruit, and then the nuts. Scrape the batter into the prepared pan and bake for 50 minutes to 1 hour, or until a skewer inserted into the middle comes out clean.

Leave in the pan for 10 minutes, then carefully run a knife between the cake and the pan and invert onto a wire rack. Turn the cake over so it is the right way up. Let cool, then dust with confectioners' sugar.

Serve in slices, with extra blackberries on the side. I like sweetened crème fraîche with it, but offer whipped cream if you like that better.

darkness and light

the soul of spain

sherry & orange caramelized fennel with goat cheese

arroz negro with romesco sauce

spanish chocolate & pedro ximénez ice cream

As soon as I get off the plane I know I'm in Madrid. I might be walking through a calm, light-filled airport (the beautiful Madrid-Barajas), but I can feel the pull of somewhere darker. It starts first with the aroma—leather, garlic, and cologne—then I hear the language. Smoking isn't as popular in Spain as it once was, but most of the men still sound as if they're on forty a day. The rich "j" sounds—formed in the back of the throat—mean conversations are made up of woody growls as much as words. (V.S. Pritchett in *The Spanish Temper* referred to these as "dry-throated gutturals," but that is only to hear the harshness and not the beauty.)

I first went to Spain to see a man about a horse. My dad was selling one—a show-jumper who had performed well at Dublin Horse Show—to a rider in Madrid. I was sixteen and had just done O-level Spanish and was, ambitiously, going along as the translator. Speaking the language didn't bother me. But the bar where we met Luis was another matter. Spain is full of brightness—the sun, its flag, flamenco dresses—but also darkness. El Greco wasn't born in Spain, but he is a painter *of* Spain. Prints of his works hung on the wall outside my school Latin classroom. Full of dark figures who seemed to emanate light even though they were somber and lugubrious, they formed my sense of the country. The literature we were studying in Spanish class was dark, too. Lorca's plays were all bitterness and repression. Machado, Spain's most famous poet, often wrote about the late afternoon, a time of shadows and melancholy. When we learned that Spaniards bought tickets for bull fights according to where they wanted to sit—in *sol o sombra*—sun or shade—it seemed entirely apt.

The bar in Madrid where we met Luis was an El Greco brought to life. Serious men lounged in old leather chairs; bottles of sherry, the color of treacle and maple syrup, were lined up behind a green tiled bar. Voices were deep; smoke and a gorgeous smell of tobacco filled the air and dust motes gave life to shafts of light. I was the only female. A trip to France was my one previous experience of "otherness" and this was much more foreign. It wasn't the Madrid of my Spanish grammar book, where Mercedes and Flores spent their afternoons boating in the Parque del Retiro. In our four days there I found it a city of cavernous bars, magisterial buildings, and terrible heat. They say that in Madrid there are *nueve meses de invierno y tres meses de infierno* (nine months of winter and three months of hell)…and the heat was infernal. I lay in bed every night and listened as they hosed the streets. Only when dawn broke was the city deemed to be clean of the previous day's dust and sweat.

The restaurants were as full of life as Machado was full of melancholy, dizzying in their noise level and energy. We sat at small tables where we were delivered plate after plate. I couldn't have dreamt up these dishes: a cold soup of almonds, bread, garlic, and olive oil; fried squid with allioli and a gash of smoked paprika; every bit of a pig that you could name (and many that you couldn't); egg-rich pastries that seemed to be from another age. I loved the food. But by the time I left Madrid, I didn't know whether I felt the same about the country.

Foreigners have been accused of painting Spain as a dark place, as a *leyenda negra*, a "black legend," full of cruel priests, inquisitors, and grief. But I think this comes from *Spanish* paintings and literature. Lorca, after all, wrote, "In Spain the dead are more alive than the dead of any other place." As I continued studying Spanish, the country's complexity became more understandable. We had a teaching assistant, Paz, from Salamanca. Franco had died in 1975 and Spain had moved, with seeming ease, to democracy. But in 1979 Paz would only talk about Franco in whispers, as if his ghost was hiding around the corners of this small Northern Irish school. She was scared of him. Democracy was only working because there was an unspoken understanding that everybody would push the Civil War, and the Franco years, away. It was a vow of silence, *el pacto del olvido*, "the pact of forgetting." I think this Spain of two halves (and also of small states—the Basque country, Catalonia—that didn't want to belong to this larger entity) reminded me of my own country. Ireland had its darkness and light, too. The Troubles had been around for my entire childhood, and there'd been "troubles" for years before that, so it was in many ways a grim place, but we, like the Spanish, were also good at enjoying ourselves and putting our best side to the world.

Paz held a small party for my Spanish class one night. We invited the other language assistants, lit a fire on the beach, and ran crazily up and down the dunes, then cooked paella back at her apartment (I'd had to look hard for large shrimp and snails and, yes, the snails were canned). We danced until we all crashed out at about 4 A.M. It was a high-octane night but, even so, Paz made sure there was a fissure of bleakness. She made us listen as she read from Ted Hughes's *Wodwo*—a collection full of feuds and destructiveness—before we fell asleep, as if we couldn't have a good time without also considering more serious things.

In the summer before I started university, I traveled around Spain, a country that still scared me, and I went *because* it scared me. Why would I have wanted the elegance of Italy, with its beautiful villas and rows of cypress trees, when I could have this difficult country instead? Ted Hughes later wrote, in *Birthday Letters*, about how Sylvia Plath hated Spain, how its "oiled anchovy faces, the African black edges" had frightened her. I empathized, though that summer was also a summer of light. The Andalusian countryside was so white—scorched by heat—it hurt my eyes; Seville was a dream of hidden courtyards, orange trees, small white-washed squares, and intricately decorated tiles. I no longer saw Spain as an El Greco but as another painting I discovered in Madrid: *La tertulia del café de Pombo*, by José Gutiérrez Solana, (part of it appears in the photograph with this menu). Spain was serious, yes, but it was a place I wanted to understand—and there was always wine and *jamón* on the table.

In contrast to the darkness, the bright side of Spain is about having a good time, about energy. Spaniards believe they have a right to enjoy themselves and they do so noisily and constantly. Food is part of this and so, too, is how Spaniards choose to consume it. Especially in Madrid, they defy normal sleeping hours. If they feel like it, they just ignore the night. You meet for dinner, but first you have to have tapas and drinks (in different locations). Dinner might not be eaten until 11 P.M., and then you party and then, finally, you go for churros. Eating and chatting can go on all night long. It's known as *trasnochar*, to "cross the night," and it's mandatory to do this and still turn up for work looking bright-eyed.

I'm not going to stretch the "darkness and light" metaphor to fit the food but *arroz negro*, black rice, which I first ate in Catalonia in my early twenties, was the most shocking and intense dish I had, at that time, ever tasted. Catalonia has the most surprising food in Spain. It balances elements and pushes them, too. There's the play of sweet with savory. (It's the Moorish legacy, and I love it most in allioli made with quince, apples, or pears. A garlic mayonnaise made with fruit? Madness.) You also see dishes that combine food from the sea and the land (*mar i muntanya*), such as the classic chicken with shrimp and pulverized chocolate, bread, nuts, and herbs. It's not surprising that Catalonia gave birth to Ferran Adrià and molecular gastronomy (it produced Gaudì, after all, and is home to the Parc Natural del Cap de Creus, an area that influenced Salvador Dalì). Adrià is about posing questions, pushing cooking to the limit, offering the unexpected. To try to capture and intensify the flavor of olives by dripping concentrated olive juice into calcium alginate to form a liquid sphere…one of the only places this could have happened is Spain. Because Spain, despite its troubled past (or perhaps because of it, as people try to reach beyond the difficult and the shaming), is focussed on the future. (You can see this in the country's architecture too. Richard Rogers has described Spain as "Europe's architectural power house.")

On the night I ate the black rice I ended up in a little coastal town on the Costa Brava, the kind of pretty place artists go to paint, where a festival was in full swing. It was both strange and thrilling—locals were wearing frightening beaked masks and dancing in the street—and everyone was eating *buñuelos* (little deep-fried clouds of dough, lighter than doughnuts, dusted with sugar). My friend and I sat in a bar drinking *cremat*, a flaming mixture of dark rum, sugar, coffee, cinnamon, and lemon peel. Set alight in a terracotta dish, the rum burns with the flavorings until only about two-thirds of the liquid remains, then it's ladled into cups of bitter coffee. It would be a daring way to end this meal, and a good way to contemplate darkness and light.

sherry & orange caramelized fennel with goat cheese

You can serve this on its own, or with other Spanish things that you've bought—*jamón ibérico de bellota* (if you're really going to town), Ortiz anchovies, slices of fried morcilla—but keep it simple. The meal is already quite rich; over-complication will spoil it. Make the fennel in advance and serve it at room temperature, though hold back the cheese, hazelnuts, and the last flourish of extra virgin olive oil until just before serving.

serves 6

2 teaspoons fennel seeds

2½ tablespoons blanched hazelnuts, halved

5 medium fennel bulbs

1 tablespoon unsalted butter

1½ tablespoons extra virgin olive oil, plus more to serve

1¼ cups medium sherry, divided

juice of ½ large orange, plus zest of 1 orange, removed with a zester

4 teaspoons granulated sugar

sea salt flakes and freshly ground black pepper

5½oz goat cheese, crumbled

Put the fennel seeds in a mortar and bash them a bit with the pestle, just to bruise them. Put the nuts in a dry skillet, place over medium heat, and toast them, stirring frequently, until they turn a shade darker and smell toasted. Set aside.

Trim the tips of the fennel bulbs, removing and reserving any little feathery fronds you see. Quarter the bulbs lengthwise and remove the coarse outer leaves. Cut each piece in half again.

Melt the butter in a large skillet and add the extra virgin olive oil. Cook the fennel pieces over medium-high heat on each side until they're golden (about 4 minutes); keep moving them around the skillet to color them more or less evenly. Add ½ cup of the sherry and the fennel seeds, then reduce the heat, cover the pan, and cook for about 7 minutes. Now pour in the orange juice and cook for another 7 minutes or so. You want the fennel to be tender but not collapsing (the wedges should keep their shape). Increase the heat, uncover the pan, and cook until the juices have almost completely disappeared.

Add the sugar to the pan and cook for about 30 seconds, turning the fennel pieces over, or until slightly caramelized. Add the rest of the sherry along with most of the orange zest and salt and pepper and cook—again turning the wedges over—until the sherry has reduced and the wedges are coated and glossy, but not too dark.

Remove the fennel to a serving plate. When you're ready to serve, sprinkle with the goat cheese, hazelnuts, remaining orange zest, and the reserved fennel fronds, then finish with more extra virgin olive oil.

arroz negro with romesco sauce

This dish marks my falling in love with the food of Catalonia (though *arroz negro* is cooked farther along the Mediterranean coast, too). I was twenty-three and blown away by allioli made with quince, raw salt cod with oranges…and this, rice as black as night, colored by squid or cuttlefish ink. *Arroz negro* is visually stunning (and transgresses our idea of what appetizing food should look like), but its appearance is not the point, really. It is deeply fishy; it tastes of darkness and the sea. You're really supposed to have allioli with it (see page 64), but I like romesco (another Catalan sauce) alongside. Or serve both; what an indulgence. In Spain this is more often made with cuttlefish, but I don't see that very often, and squid works just fine.

serves 6

for the romesco sauce
3 small red bell peppers, halved and seeded

2 medium tomatoes, halved

6 garlic cloves, unpeeled

regular olive oil

sea salt and black pepper

⅓ cup blanched hazelnuts

¼ cup blanched almonds

1 teaspoon sweet Spanish paprika

½ cup extra virgin olive oil, or to taste

4 teaspoons sherry vinegar

for the rice and squid
2lb squid, cleaned weight

¼ cup regular olive oil

1 onion, finely chopped

3 garlic cloves, finely chopped

4 plum tomatoes, chopped

1lb Calasparra rice

8 squid ink sachets

8 cups hot fish stock

3½ tablespoons flat-leaf parsley leaves

juice of ½ to 1 lemon, to taste

Preheat the oven to 350°F.

To make the romesco, put the peppers and tomatoes into a small roasting pan. Tuck the garlic in under them (the cloves can burn, so it's best if they're protected by the vegetables) and pour regular olive oil over everything. Season and cook for 30 to 40 minutes, or until the vegetables are soft and slightly caramelized. Let cool. You can remove the skin from the peppers, but I rarely bother; I like the taste of it when it's slightly blistered. Squeeze the soft pulp from the garlic cloves and discard their skins.

Toast both types of nut in a dry skillet until they're golden all over, but be careful not to burn them; you need to toss them frequently. Let cool.

Put the nuts into a food processor and blitz. Add the other ingredients and process until smooth. Taste and adjust the seasoning if you need to. You may want to add a little water, or more extra virgin olive oil, if it seems too thick. Cover and set aside.

Now remove the wings from the squid. Cut the bodies open down one side, then cut them into slices about ¼ inch in thickness. Slice any large tentacles in half, too. Heat 2 to 3 tablespoons of the regular olive oil in a heavy 12 inch sauté pan. Once it's hot, quickly sauté the squid for about 30 seconds, then lift it out and set aside.

Add more regular olive oil to the pan if you need it and sauté the onion gently until soft and translucent. Stir in the garlic and tomatoes and cook for a couple of minutes, then reduce the heat to low and cook until you have a soft, thick mixture. It will take about 10 minutes.

Add the rice. Squeeze the squid ink into the stock and add this to the pan with the squid. Season lightly and stir in the parsley. Bring to a boil, then reduce the heat to a gentle simmer. Let the rice cook for about 25 minutes, by which time the stock should have been fully absorbed. Keep an eye on the mixture and add a little water if it's in danger of becoming completely dry. Don't stir it, except when checking what's going on at the bottom of the pan. Add some lemon juice and taste for seasoning. Serve with the romesco sauce.

spanish chocolate & pedro ximénez ice cream

Chocolate and Pedro Ximénez sherry are a perfect pair. The two ingredients enhance each other so well it's hard to know where one flavor ends and the other begins. People always eat this slowly, savoring every raisiny mouthful. Don't be tempted to add more sherry than stated in the recipe, or you'll end up with an ice cream that contains too much alcohol and won't freeze properly. This is already a soft-scoop ice cream; make it the day before, leave it in the freezer overnight, and serve straight from there. It doesn't need any time to soften.

serves 6 to 8

1¾ cups whole milk

½ cup heavy cream

½ cup superfine sugar

3 large egg yolks

7oz dark chocolate, 70 percent cocoa solids, broken into small pieces

½ teaspoon vanilla extract

1 scant cup Pedro Ximénez sherry

Heat the milk, cream, and superfine sugar together until just below boiling, stirring a little to help the sugar dissolve. Beat the egg yolks in a bowl with a wooden spoon. Slowly pour the cream and milk mixture onto the eggs, stirring the whole time. Pour this into a clean heavy saucepan and place over low heat, stirring all the time. The mixture must not boil or the egg yolks will scramble, but you do need the custard to thicken enough to coat the back of a spoon; if you run your finger along the spoon it should leave a clear channel. It might take 15 minutes for it to thicken sufficiently.

Immediately take the pan off the heat and add the chocolate, about 10 pieces at a time. Stir to help it melt. It's really important that the chocolate melts completely. At first it won't and you may panic a little, but keep stirring until you get there. Do not return the pan to the heat.

Pour into a bowl, cover, and place the mixture in the fridge for a few hours to chill (overnight is even better). Only when the mixture is chilled should you stir in the vanilla and sherry.

Churn in an ice-cream machine, or transfer to a shallow container and put in the freezer. If you're using the manual method, take the ice cream out and churn it—either using an electric hand mixer or by putting the mixture in a food processor—3 times during the freezing process. Do this first after about 1 hour, when the mixture is setting around the edges, then at 2-hour intervals, until it's frozen and smooth. Cover with a lid, or with plastic wrap or parchment paper, between each churning, and when you store it.

monsieur matuchet plays the piano

a dinner from south-west france

apéritif agenais

onion, spinach & bleu d'auvergne tart

roast quail with *aillade*

wild mushrooms & potatoes | green salad with hazelnut dressing

fig & honey cake

Backpacking was never my thing. In my early twenties, when friends were setting off for long stints exploring Asia, I was planning intricate journeys around regional France. *The Good Hotel Guide*—most of whose hotels I couldn't afford—was my bedtime reading, along with Patricia Wells's *Food Lover's Guide to France*. I studied the descriptions of my favorite hotels so often that, these days, I'm not sure which I stayed in and which I didn't. (If you read about a place often enough, I find, you might as well have visited.)

The Lot Valley and the Dordogne—an area which seemed to have more *plus belles villages de France* than any other—became my dream destination. I wanted cassoulet and walnuts, duck confit and prunes. Driving down through France with my then-boyfriend, finally on our way there, the people we met confirmed that we were heading for the right place. "*On mange bien, là-bas,*" they said. The colors changed as we traveled, until we were surrounded by shades of honey, ocher, terracotta, and the green-gold of burrs.

Our first night was spent in St-Cirq-Lapopie, a medieval *village-perché*, in a hotel just under André Breton's house. The bedroom was tiny; it had uneven whitewashed walls and a small window that looked out onto the Lot below. The ceiling, a chalky azure painted with little gold stars, was so enchanting it nearly took precedence over dinner. I'll just stay here, I thought, and lie on the white bedcover looking at the stars and thinking about walnuts.

Monsier Matuchet—the hotel's owner and an Alain Delon lookalike—showed us into the dining room. On a rough-hewn table there were sweet-smelling Charentais melons, a huge ham, bottles of walnut oil and Armagnac, jars of duck confit, and a big earthenware bowl of booze-soaked prunes.

All the food came from nearby and made you realize that the countryside here wasn't just beautiful, it was hardworking. I stopped thinking of the place as postcard bucolic and started to see what anchored it. The menu—which Monsieur Matuchet talked us through—was one of those perfect short affairs you get in France that have only two choices at every course. Even though it was early September, and summer was still hanging around, the kitchen was in full autumnal swing: there were salads of smoked duck and wild mushrooms with duck gizzards, a pork and bean stew, duck breast with the potent walnut and garlic sauce (*aillade*), figs with hazelnut ice cream.

Monsieur Matuchet, creator of star-speckled ceilings, was also in charge of the kitchen. It was honest, unflashy cooking, yet the cuisine of south-west France is so burdened by the image of foie gras and cassoulet—the first deemed too luxurious, the other too gutsy for modern stomachs as well as too time-consuming to make—that it's not raved about by home cooks outside France in the way that, say, Provençal cooking is. It's seen as heavy and old-fashioned. But when autumn comes round, I think about Monsieur Matuchet and the rich-but-homely food he produced that night.

The American food writer Paula Wolfert has written about "front-of-the-mouth food"—complex, innovative dishes that dazzle but whose charms quickly evaporate—and also its opposite, "evolved" food, cooking based on ingredients that have a natural affinity with one another, dishes that honor the spirit of a particular region. Evolved cooking is what you find in south-west France, and it encompasses far more than foie gras and cassoulet. Duck legs with prunes, garlic-studded pork, Armagnac-scented apple tarts…these make for better eating on the cool, gauzy days of autumn than any plate of roasted Mediterranean vegetables. They are dishes with length and depth of flavor.

I wasn't surprised that most of the people in the dining room that night were French. The only other tourists, an American couple with wide-brimmed hats that they wore to dinner, kept smiling at us as if to acknowledge our shared luck in finding this gem of a place.

Monsier Matuchet's menu was do-able, just as is the one that follows. I know this because, as soon as the main courses were served, Monsieur M was able to leave the kitchen and show off another of his talents. He took to the piano and played jazz (of course he did). It made me love the place all the more. The Americans smiled broadly.

apéritif agenais

You need to make *pruneaux au Monbazillac* for this, and well in advance (at least a month), so this is a treat that you need to plan ahead. The best prunes are usually unpitted and should be left that way, so you don't squash them. Warn your guests there are pits in their boozy prunes, though.

fills a 1-quart jar

for the prunes
1lb 2oz good-quality prunes, preferably from Agen

⅔ cup *eau de vie de prune* (or vodka)

⅔ cup light rum

⅓ cup granulated sugar

1¼ cups Monbazillac (or another rich, sweet white wine)

to serve
chilled champagne

Put the prunes into a saucepan. Pour on the *eau de vie* and rum and gently bring to just under boiling. Immediately take the pan off the heat and leave the prunes to soak overnight.

The next day, strain the prunes and return the alcohol to the pan. Add the sugar and heat, stirring to help the sugar dissolve. Put the prunes into a sterilized 1-quart jar (see page 86) and add the boozy syrup. Top off with Monbazillac to cover generously. Seal. Let stand for at least 1 month before trying (these will keep for years).

To make the aperitif, put 1 prune in a champagne flute. Cover with spoonfuls of the syrup from the jar and slowly top off with champagne. Provide long spoons, so your guests can eat the prunes.

onion, spinach & bleu d'auvergne tart

You can offer squares of this while people are chatting with the *apéritif Agenais* before you all sit down, or serve slices on plates with a few salad greens and a dressing based on hazelnut oil (see page 187).

serves 6

1½lb spinach leaves

3 tablespoons extra virgin olive oil, plus 2 tablespoons

2¼lb onions, very finely sliced

sea salt flakes and freshly ground black pepper

leaves from 4 thyme sprigs

3 garlic cloves, crushed

1 tablespoon light brown sugar

½ tablespoon apple cider vinegar, plus more to taste

½ tablespoon balsamic vinegar (regular or white), plus more to taste

all-purpose flour, to dust

1lb 2oz ready-made puff pastry

3½oz bleu d'Auvergne cheese, crumbled, or another blue cheese (not too salty)

Wash the spinach leaves, then place them in a large saucepan, cover, and cook over medium-low heat in the water that clings to them. It will look like a lot of spinach, but it really cooks down. Keep turning the leaves over so that they all get a chance to be in contact with the bottom of the pan. It will take about 7 minutes to cook this quantity of spinach. Pour into a colander and let drain and cool.

Put the 3 tablespoons of extra virgin olive oil into a large, heavy saucepan, add the onions, and cook over medium heat for about 7 minutes, until they are losing their rawness and beginning to turn pale gold. Add salt and pepper and a splash of water, cover the pan, reduce the heat to low, and sweat the onions for about 1 hour. During this time, they become really soft. Keep checking to make sure they are moist enough, adding a splash of water every so often if necessary.

Add the thyme and garlic and cook for another 15 minutes. Add the sugar and vinegars, then increase the heat and cook the onions—with the lid off—until they are deep gold and all excess liquid has boiled off. The mixture should be sweet-savory, so adjust by adding a little more vinegar if it's too sweet. Adjust the seasoning if needed, as well.

Preheat the oven to 375°F.

Lightly flour a work surface and roll out the pastry to almost cover a 16 x 12 inch baking sheet. It doesn't need to be perfect, in fact a few rough edges looks better. Bake for 25 minutes. The pastry will puff up in the middle, but don't worry. Take it out of the oven and bash the puffy middle bit down with the back of a wooden spoon.

While the pastry is cooking, squeeze the water out of the spinach, either using your hands or by pressing fistfuls between 2 dinner plates. Chop the spinach coarsely and sauté it in the 2 tablespoons of extra virgin olive oil until it is warmed through and covered in oil, seasoning well.

Spread the onions on the pastry, leaving a 1½-inch rim around the edge, then put the spinach on top, flattening it. Season and put back in the oven. Cook for another 15 minutes, scattering it with the cheese about 7 minutes before the end of cooking time.

roast quail with *aillade*

This is gorgeous. Even though there are two sauces to make—the *aillade*, a walnut sauce from south-west France, and a sauce made with the quail cooking juices—it's worth it. Traditional *aillade* has more garlic, though I find that version rather rasping, so I've cut down the quantity. If you don't like quail, you can use one poussin per person instead. Poussin need to be cooked at 375°F for about 45 minutes. Roast duck breasts or legs are great, too.

serves 6

for the quails
2 bay leaves, crumbled

leaves from 4 thyme sprigs

finely grated zest of ½ small unwaxed lemon

¼ cup brandy

sea salt flakes and freshly ground black pepper

extra virgin olive oil

12 quail

½ stick unsalted butter, cut into 12 small pieces

1½ cups dry white vermouth

2 cups well-flavored chicken stock

for the aillade
2 large garlic cloves, peeled

¾ cup shelled walnuts

⅔ cup walnut oil

1 tablespoon finely chopped flat-leaf parsley leaves

Marinate the quails the day before. Mix the herbs, zest, brandy, salt, and pepper with 6 tablespoons of the extra virgin olive oil. Season the birds and spoon some marinade inside. Roll the outsides in the rest of the marinade, put into a large roasting pan, cover, and chill.

For the *aillade*, crush the garlic, walnuts, and a little salt with a mortar and pestle. Once the nuts are well pounded, add the walnut oil in a thin stream, as if making mayonnaise. Stir in 2 tablespoons of warm water (sometimes I use chicken stock, as it gives it real depth). Add pepper and the chopped parsley and set aside.

Preheat the oven to 400°F. To cook the quail, wipe any herbs from the breast area of the birds. Heat the remaining 3 tablespoons of extra virgin olive oil in a large skillet and, when really hot, quickly brown the birds, in batches, all over, especially on the breasts. You only want to color the outsides, not cook the meat.

Stick a small nugget of butter inside each bird and put into 1 large roasting pan (or 2), without crowding them together. Roast for 15 to 20 minutes, depending on whether you like the meat a little pink, adding one-quarter of the vermouth halfway through cooking time.

Remove the birds to a warmed platter and cover. Put the roasting pan over high heat and add the rest of the vermouth. Bring to a boil, then let it reduce until you have about ⅔ cup left. Add the stock and boil until you have a slightly syrupy sauce, enough to drizzle a couple of tablespoons over each serving of quail.

Put 2 quail on each of 6 warmed plates, drizzle each with some of the reduced sauce, and spoon some of the *aillade* alongside. Serve with the wild mushrooms and potatoes on page 187, as well as the hazelnut oil salad, if you didn't serve that with the tart.

wild mushrooms & potatoes

Make sure to cook the mushrooms until their moisture has evaporated and they're quite dry. You don't want this dish to be soggy.

serves 6

2 to 3 tablespoons regular olive oil, divided

1lb cooked waxy potatoes, thickly sliced

sea salt flakes and freshly ground black pepper

1lb wild or cultivated mushrooms, sliced quite thickly

2 tablespoons unsalted butter

handful of finely chopped flat-leaf parsley leaves

Heat 1 tablespoon of the regular olive oil in a large skillet and fry the potatoes (you may have to do this in 2 batches), seasoning as you go. Remove the potatoes once they are golden.

Add another 1 tablespoon of oil and sauté half the mushrooms over a brisk heat. You want a good color all over. Season. Keep cooking over fairly high heat until all the moisture has gone (mushrooms give out a lot and you need it to evaporate). Scrape them into a bowl and fry the other half in the same way. Return all the mushrooms to the pan and add the butter, to give a really good flavor. Now return the potatoes to the pan, toss everything together until it has all warmed through, check the seasoning, add the parsley, and serve.

green salad with hazelnut dressing

One of the most important parts of this meal…yet it requires no cooking. A salad after the main course is one of the best things about a meal in France. When you're making the vinaigrette here, make sure to taste and taste again; seasoning and balance is all. I like the bit of sweetness a dash of crème de cassis brings, but you don't have to use it.

serves 6

¾ teaspoon Dijon mustard

½ tablespoon red wine vinegar

1 tablespoon extra virgin olive oil (fruity, not a grassy Tuscan one)

3 tablespoons hazelnut oil

¼ to ½ teaspoon crème de cassis

7oz mâche, baby spinach, or a mixture

To make the dressing, put the mustard into a small bowl, add the vinegar, and season with sea salt flakes and freshly ground black pepper. Whisk in both oils with a small fork and add the cassis to taste. Check the seasoning.

Pick through the salad leaves, discarding any that are limp. Put the rest in a bowl and toss with the dressing.

fig & honey cake

Rich and autumnal. Serve in slim slices, preferably while the cake is still warm.

serves 8

¾ cup Port, Marsala, or Madeira

juice of ½ lemon, plus a broad strip of unwaxed lemon zest, plus the finely grated zest of ⅓ unwaxed lemon

1 rosemary sprig

¾ cup liquid honey, divided

12 figs (though it may take more, depending on size)

1½ sticks unsalted butter, softened, plus more for the pan

2 cups all-purpose flour, plus more for the pan

¼ cup unpacked soft light brown sugar

½ teaspoon vanilla extract

3 large eggs, at room temperature, lightly beaten

2 teaspoons baking powder

pinch of sea salt flakes

½ cup ground walnuts or hazelnuts

crème fraîche, to serve

Put the Port, Masala, or Madeira, lemon juice, the strip of zest, and the rosemary into a pan with half the honey and bring gently to a boil. Meanwhile, snip the stalks off the figs and halve them lengthwise. Poach the figs in the honey mixture for about 5 minutes, or until they are just slightly soft, turning them over once during this time. (The figs will be cooked more later, but this just helps impart some of their flavor to the liquid.) Lift the figs out of the poaching liquid and let them cool in a single layer, each set apart from the next.

Boil the poaching liquor until it is has thickened a little and is becoming slightly syrupy (it will thicken more as it cools). Set aside.

Preheat the oven to 350°F. Butter a 9-inch springform cake pan, line the bottom with nonstick parchment paper, then lightly flour the pan and tap out the excess.

Beat the butter and sugar until light and fluffy, then beat in the other half of the honey, plus the vanilla and finely grated lemon zest. Gradually add the eggs, a little at a time, beating well after each addition. Sift the flour, baking powder, and salt together. Fold this in, along with the ground walnuts or hazelnuts, until well combined. Scrape into your prepared pan (it will seem as if you don't have much batter, but this is a rich cake and shouldn't be too deep). Carefully set the drained figs on top, cut-side up. Bake for 45 minutes. A skewer inserted into the center of the cake (avoiding the figs) should come out clean.

Leave the cake in the pan for about 15 minutes, then carefully release the latch and remove the sides, peeling the nonstick parchment paper off of the bottom. Paint the top of the cake with the reserved syrup and let this settle for a while before serving. This is good served slightly warm (though it will be more crumbly). Offer some crème fraîche, as it needs a bit of sharpness alongside.

in my own backyard

a british-irish sunday lunch

smoked eel with beet rémoulade & guinness bread

partridges with red cabbage, blackberries & star anise

seville orange tart

It's hard for me to listen to Van Morrison's song "Coney Island." It's not about Coney Island in New York, but about a little island in Lough Neagh in Northern Ireland. It relays the small details of a Sunday drive round that area in autumn sunshine, picking up the Sunday papers, doing a bit of birdwatching. As Van says, "the *craic* was good." The line that gets me is this: "Stop off at Ardglass for a couple of jars of mussels and some potted herrings, in case we get famished before dinner." Van growls through this—half-singing, half-speaking—in his untouched Northern Irish accent. And there is my father, summed up in a song.

Most years we went to Dublin on vacation, and the first stopping point was a place where dad bought cockles and mussels. He ate them in the car, from little paper cartons. The shellfish stop indicated that we were really on vacation, that we were going to the magical south of Ireland, and that dad was happy. Food marked this vacation excitement, but also a joy taken in life. "Here, try it!" he would often command, holding out a forkful of some new flavor and texture, willing us to be more adventurous. My dad is only seventy-eight—not old—but I know that one day I will listen to "Coney Island" and that it will be unbearable.

My mum was the cook in our family. I am of a generation when that was a mother's job. When dad cooked—flipping marinated chicken thighs on the barbecue, messing up the entire kitchen making chicken liver pâté—it stood out; it was something special. It seems unfair, therefore, that my dad's attitude to and love for food influenced me perhaps even more than my mum's…but it did. When he went away on a trip, it was always food he brought back: jars of Scandinavian herrings, shining silver behind glass, bought hurriedly at airport duty-free; links of fat sausages from Buckley's in Dublin, which he would triumphantly produce from his briefcase (we always had those on Christmas morning); silky smoked salmon. He picked up wild stuff, too, from friends. Big salmon—so fresh they looked as if they might still leap—and pheasants in the feather (though I hated those, with their beady eyes and soft, small-boned bodies).

When we went on our first foreign vacation—to Portugal—we had one night in a "posh" restaurant. The rest of us ordered dishes we recognized. Dad ordered salt cod fritters and cataplana. We marveled at this big copper spaceship of pork and clams (what an odd combination, what a dish), which he emptied, tackling every last clam with his big hands. At every turn, he urged us to try the new, the unusual.

I know that my dad's love of food really formed me. From my mother I learnt skills. From my father I learned to taste the world. This menu is for my dad. From the smoked eel to the orange tart, he would eat it greedily.

smoked eel with beet rémoulade & guinness bread

This is also good made with smoked trout, as the sweet-bitter Guinness bread is great with smoky flavors, but remember the recipe and make it to serve with cheese, too.

serves 6

for the bread

2 tablespoons unsalted butter, cut into small cubes, plus more for the pan

1⅔ cups whole wheat flour

⅔ cup all-purpose flour

¼ cup rolled oats, plus extra for the top

1¼ teaspoons baking soda

sea salt flakes

2 tablespoons soft dark brown sugar

⅓ cup Guinness stout

2 tablespoons dark molasses

1 scant cup buttermilk

for the rémoulade

¼ cup home-made or good-quality store-bought mayonnaise

¼ cup crème fraîche

1 teaspoon Dijon mustard

3 teaspoons freshly grated horseradish, or to taste

freshly ground black pepper

juice of ½ lemon

7oz celery root, peeled

7oz raw beets, peeled

to serve

7oz smoked eel

dill sprigs

Preheat the oven to 350°F. Butter a small loaf pan (mine is 7½ x 3½ x 2 inches).

Mix the flours and oatmeal, the baking soda, and ½ teaspoon salt in a bowl. Rub in the butter with your fingertips. Stir in the sugar.

Combine the Guinness, molasses, and buttermilk in a measuring cup. Make a well in the center of the dry ingredients. Gradually pour in the liquid, mixing with a butter knife as you go. Don't over-mix or you'll end up with a wet dough. Pour into the prepared pan and sprinkle with rolled oats.

Bake for 40 to 50 minutes. To test if it's cooked, remove from the pan and tap the bottom. If it sounds hollow, it's ready. If not, bake for a little longer, but don't overcook it or it'll be dry. Invert onto a wire rack and let cool.

Mix together the mayonnaise, crème fraîche, mustard, and horseradish. Season to taste.

Put the lemon juice and a little water into a large bowl. Cut the celery root into fine matchsticks, adding them to the water as you go, to prevent discoloration. Cut the beets into the same-sized matchsticks. Quickly drain the celery root and pat it dry with a clean dish cloth, then add it to the mayonnaise mixture with the beets.

Slice the bread, then halve each slice. Butter lightly, and put some rémoulade and a piece of eel on each half slice. Add a little dill.

partridges with red cabbage, blackberries & star anise

The season for blackberries, which often runs into October in Northern Ireland, only extends to mid-September in England, while gray partridges are available from the beginning of September to the beginning of February. I love the combination so much, however, that I use either wild berries I've picked and stashed in the freezer, or the cultivated blackberries that seem to be available for most of the year now.

serves 6

¾ stick unsalted butter, at room temperature, divided, plus more for the parchment paper

½ tablespoon regular olive oil

2 red onions, finely sliced

2 garlic cloves, crushed

1 teaspoon ground pumpkin pie spice

2 small star anise

1 red cabbage, cored and shredded

¼ cup unpacked soft light brown sugar, or to taste

⅓ cup balsamic vinegar, or to taste

sea salt flakes and freshly ground black pepper

6 dressed red-legged or Hungarian partridges, each barded with (wrapped in) 1 slice unsmoked bacon

6 juniper berries

1¼ cups blackberries

2 tablespoons crème de mûre or crème de cassis

Heat 2 tablespoons of the butter and all the regular olive oil in a heavy saucepan and gently sauté the onions until soft (10 to 15 minutes). Don't let them brown. Add the garlic, pumpkin pie spice, and star anise and cook for a couple of minutes, then add the cabbage, sugar, and balsamic vinegar and season. Turn the cabbage over in the butter, cooking gently for about 2 minutes. Bring to a boil, then reduce the heat to very low, cover, and cook gently for about 50 minutes, turning the cabbage over every so often. It should be nice and soft.

If you are preparing this a day ahead—and it does improve if it spends a night in the fridge—stop the cooking now, let cool, cover, and chill. Reheat it gently the next day, when the partridges are nearly ready.

To cook the partridges, preheat the oven to 410°F. Crush the juniper berries and mix them with the remaining butter. Put a little nugget of butter inside each bird then rub the rest all over them. Truss each bird with kitchen string. Season and put the birds into a roasting pan, lying on one side. Roast for 8 minutes. Turn onto their other sides and roast for another 8 minutes. Generously butter a piece of parchment paper—large enough to cover the partridges in the roasting pan—set the on top of the birds and return to the oven for another 15 minutes. Remove from the oven, turn the birds over onto their breasts, and cover with foil and a few old dish cloths so they can rest.

Reheat the cabbage, adding the blackberries and crème de mûre or crème de cassis. Cook uncovered for a couple of minutes to reduce the juices and soften the berries. The cabbage should be glossy and moist, not watery. Taste for seasoning and sweet-sour balance, adding vinegar or sugar, if you like (go carefully). Pick out the star anise.

Serve the roast partridges with the cabbage and some puréed celery root, or potatoes mashed with celery root.

seville orange tart

This isn't quick or easy—each component takes patience and care—but it's glorious. Keep a careful eye on the orange slices; they require vigilance, as ovens rarely stay at an even temperature. You don't want them to get dried out; they should be sticky and tender. Use navel oranges when Sevilles aren't in season.

serves 6 to 8

for the pastry
1 stick chilled unsalted butter, chopped

¾ cup confectioners' sugar

3 medium egg yolks, divided

2 cups all-purpose flour, plus more to dust

pinch of sea salt flakes

½ tablespoon milk

for the roast orange slices
3 thin-skinned, seedless oranges, cut into thin, round slices (discard the ends)

juice of 3 oranges

½ cup superfine sugar, divided, plus more if needed

To make the pastry, beat the butter and confectioners' sugar together until creamy, then beat in 2 of the egg yolks, 1 at a time. Mix in the flour and salt until the mixture comes together in a ball. Place on a floured work surface and knead briefly until smooth, but don't overwork it. Seal in plastic wrap and chill for 30 minutes in the fridge.

For the roasted oranges, preheat the oven to 350°F. Layer the slices in a gratin dish, pour on the juice, and sprinkle with 2 tablespoons of the superfine sugar. Cover with foil and bake for 1 hour, or until the peel is soft. Remove the foil, transfer them to a roasting pan in a single layer, sprinkle with the rest of the sugar, and cook for 30 to 40 minutes until almost all the juice evaporates and the slices are sticky and slightly singed. Add a little more sugar if they aren't singeing, but don't take them too far; they should stay moist. Let cool.

When the pastry has chilled for 30 minutes, roll it out on a lightly floured surface to ⅛ inch thick and use it to line a 8½-inch tart pan with a removable bottom. Let the pastry hang over the edges, keeping

for the filling

1 cup Seville orange juice (if you can't get this, use regular orange juice and replace about ¼ cup with lemon juice)

½ cup superfine sugar

4 medium eggs, lightly beaten

⅔ cup heavy cream

finely grated zest of 4 oranges

any surplus. Prick the bottom with the tines of a fork. Put in the freezer, or the coldest part of the fridge, for 1 hour. Whisk together the orange juice and superfine sugar for the filling; the sugar should dissolve. Add the rest of the ingredients for the filling.

Fill the pastry crust with crumpled nonstick parchment paper and pie weights. Bake for 15 minutes. Remove the paper and pie weights, then bake for 5 minutes. If there are cracks, fill them in with leftover pastry; it's important there are no holes or the filling will leak out. Carefully trim excess pastry from the edges. Brush the crust with the remaining egg yolk mixed with the milk. Return to the oven for a couple of minutes: this seals the shell so the custard doesn't make it soggy. Let cool.

Reduce the oven temperature to 325°F. When the oven has reached this temperature, pour the filling into the crust and bake for 50 minutes to 1 hour. The top should be set but still slightly wobbly in the middle, but it continues to cook once out of the oven. Let cool. Top with the roast orange slices to serve.

the moon and the bonfire (and the hazelnuts)

good things from piedmont

pasta with white truffles

beef cheeks in red wine with polenta

bonet

Piedmont is famous for truffles and Barolo wine, but they're not the reason I went there. I read Cesare Pavese's *The Moon and the Bonfire* in my early thirties; it's not cheerful, but the Piedmontese landscape, almost a character in the novel, cures all ills and food connects everyone to it. Those who live there hold the place "in their bones, like wine and polenta." Pavese comes from Piedmont, from La Morra (a village I love). Like Seamus Heaney, he has his feet in the soil and his nose in the air. When I read, in one of his poems, "the air's raw with fog, you drink it in sips like grappa," I had to go. I like fog. I like those layers of mist hanging over vineyards you see in photographs of Piedmont. In reality it's more beautiful. I first went in October when there's a soothing stillness and the afternoons, especially if you're walking among fruit trees (there are lots of orchards and hazelnut groves, as well as vineyards), smell of mulch and apples so ripe they're almost fermenting.

The Piedmontese are taciturn, industrious, modest, the opposite of our stereotypical idea of Italians. The place feels well-heeled. Groups of middle-aged men, wearing thick jackets and soft scarves you want to stroke, sit outside bars drinking Barolo. It looks as if women get their hair done every week. When I had dinner there one New Year's Eve, a dog—beloved pet of the family at the next table—wore a pearl choker round her neck. The wine—specifically those from the nebbiolo grape (big, aromatic, and reminiscent of tar, roses, and wood smoke)—has brought money to the region, and wine and food and work are taken seriously. (I usually drink Dolcetto, also from Piedmont; it's less expensive than Barolo, has a touch of bitterness and the dark lushness of black cherries.)

There are plenty of gourmet restaurants—Piedmont is regarded as the gastronomic center of Italy—but I'm never looking for complicated stuff, and certainly not "inventiveness." One of the joys here is that you can take simple (if sometimes expensive) ingredients and turn them into unbelievable richness:

partridges with wild mushrooms, *fonduta*—a cheese fondue made with egg yolks and milk—chocolate-stuffed pears baked in red wine. They love beef, butter, cream, and cheese. Risotto and polenta are more common than pasta, though they do have their own thin egg pasta, *tajarin*. They use my favorite olive oil—the buttery stuff from Liguria—and, despite being landlocked, anchovies are a big deal. Piedmont's position on the salt route, which winds its way from the sea at Liguria to the north, ensured that cured anchovies came to the area. Because of this, *bagna cauda*, an array of vegetables served with a bowl of anchovies melting to a purée in warm olive oil and butter (and piqued with garlic) is served everywhere. To have both anchovies and wild mushrooms in the same meal…that's some kind of heaven. Then there are the nuts. At a small market one morning in La Morra, I tasted Piedmontese hazelnuts, and hazelnut paste, and the most exquisite chocolate and hazelnut spread. People will tell you where hazelnuts are best—Spain or France or Turkey—but you haven't tasted hazelnuts until you've tasted them here. Sweet and singing and intense, every hazelnut I eat is compared to the ones I can get in La Morra (and usually found lacking). And then, of course, there are the truffles.

I'd always been an inverted snob when it came to truffles. They were, I reasoned, out of the reach of most people, so I would just leave them. It's not that I don't believe in spending money on food, it's more that I'm suspicious of anything with a really high price tag, or that smacks of braggadocio and posturing. Were truffles really wonderful, or just a vehicle for bragging?

Then I found myself, six years ago, sitting in an empty bar drinking a macchiato and waiting for my *trifolao*. Beppe, handsome, wild-haired, lots of useful pockets in his coat (which is what a truffle hunter needs), drove me to his special place with his equally wild-haired *lagotto*, Luna. Truffles are something of a miracle. A fruiting body of a fungus that grows underground, its web of filaments binds itself to the roots of trees, then feeds off it. In Piedmont the trees that "host" truffles are oak, linden, hazel, poplar, and beech, and the white Alba truffles here are the most fragrant and sought after in the world. To fruit, they need the right degree of porosity in the soil around them, the right climate, the right amount of rainfall. Beppe and I scramble up and down small escarpments under trees, occasionally slipping on the damp ground. "Vai, vai, Luna!" he urges, making gentle clucking sounds that remind me of my dad coaxing horses. Luna starts to scrape frenziedly at the earth, busy with snout and paws. Beppe pulls her back firmly, giving her a biscuit (her reward), and strikes at the earth with a small pick until he pulls out a clod. Before the soil is brushed off you can smell it: beef, Parmesan, fungi, sweat, a briny seasidey whiff, like oysters…and sex. He hands me a truffle the size of a walnut and I breathe it in. I'd scoffed at the idea of truffles being a drug, but I don't want to give it back. I close my eyes, breathe it in again. Now, wherever Luna runs, I'm right behind her. Even the faint scent—which you get as soon as the dog starts to paw at the ground—can be picked up quickly; my nose is attuned.

Later, we study different sizes and types of white truffle. The most prized are as smooth as pebbles and spherical, others are lumpy. Red-tinged ones are from oaks; ivory specimens usually from poplars.

To experience them being shaved onto warm buttery *tajarin* is even better than that first scent on the hunt. The more a truffle's surface area is exposed to the air, the stronger the aroma, and that's why you shave them thinly. The truffle falls in fine translucent slices, like damp slivers of air-dried ham or parchment, and I eat. On the rest of the trip I endeavor to be near truffles. Even if I'm not going to eat them—and I can't at every meal, they're too expensive—I sit by the truffle station in restaurants. This is usually a small table spread with a cloth, with a few scented nuggets sitting under a glass dome.

I had believed that once I'd seen the Northern Lights I could strike them off my list. It's not true, and it's not true of white truffles either. Both make you slightly crazy with wonder. You simply want more. I don't buy truffles often, just once every couple of years, though I always eat them when I'm in Piedmont. A small truffle is the price of a pair of shoes, yes, but I'll forgo other luxuries in order to have them. I crave them and think about them when I'm not there, along with the hazelnuts, the walks among the apple trees, the *bagna cauda*, and the Piedmontese fog. Not all addictions are bad; some are life-enriching.

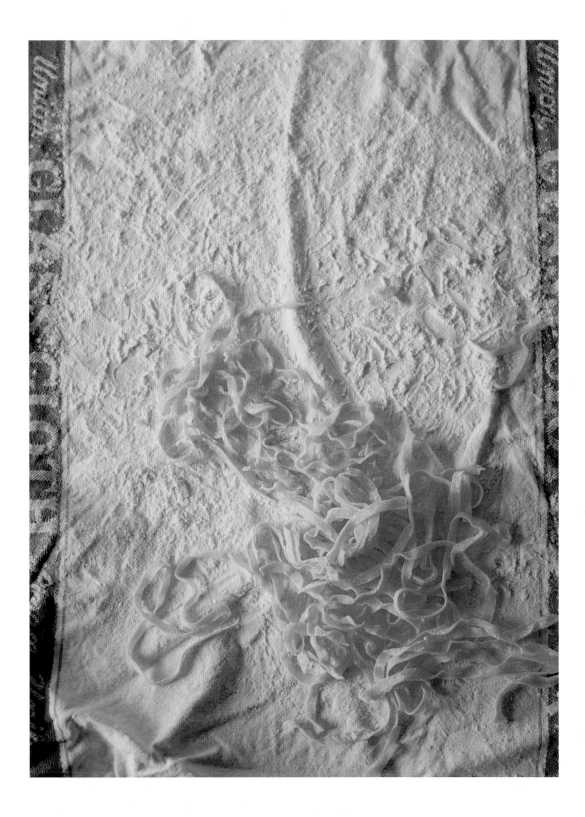

pasta with white truffles

This is not something to make for the first time when you have friends coming for dinner. I am not going to lie. You need to practice making pasta. Do it for the first time when you're not under any pressure and you have an afternoon to play with.

serves 6

2½ cups Italian type "oo" flour, plus more to dust

3 large or 4 medium eggs

sea salt flakes

1 stick unsalted butter

1¼ cups grated Parmesan cheese, plus more to serve

1 white Alba truffle (a size just smaller than a table tennis ball will do)

Place the flour into a bowl—or onto a work surface—and make a well in the center. Break the eggs into the well and, using the fingers of one hand, gradually incorporate the flour into the eggs. Put the dough onto a lightly floured surface and knead for 6 to 8 minutes. The kneading is really important, so do it properly. The dough should be smooth and slightly elastic. It should also spring back when you prod it with a finger. Seal in plastic wrap and let rest in the fridge for 1 hour.

To cut the pasta, using a hand-cranked machine, lightly flour the work surface and set up a pasta machine. Cut the dough into 3 pieces. Set the pasta machine to its widest opening. Shape and flatten the first piece of dough to fit the machine and feed it through 4 times, turning and folding it over each time. Continue, adjusting the width of the opening by moving down one setting at a time and feeding the pasta through once, until you get to the penultimate setting (don't go right to the last setting, as it is too thin for tagliatelle). As you complete the rolling, put each sheet of pasta on the floured table.

Trim each piece of pasta to a neat rectangle, then feed it through the machine to make tagliatelle. Repeat with the rest. Let the pasta dry a little by spreading the strips out on nonstick parchment paper—or a floured dish cloth—for about 15 minutes.

Fill a very large pot with water and bring it to a boil. Add salt. Add the pasta and boil for about 2 minutes. Check a piece: the middle should be cooked. If it is raw, cook for a bit longer.

Lightly drain, reserving a little of the cooking water, and return the pasta to the pan. (This moisture in the pan will form the basis of the sauce.) Add the butter in pieces, shaking the pan to emulsify the water. The resulting buttery sauce should coat the pasta, but if it seems dry add a little of the reserved cooking water. Season. Gently stir in the Parmesan. Shave half the truffle over the pasta. Serve in warmed bowls, with a little more shaved truffle, and offer more Parmesan on the side.

beef cheeks in red wine with polenta

The beef here is very rich, so it can stretch to serve eight. You can make it the day before, which actually improves it. Polenta divides people. I never liked it until I had the slow-cooked type. It has a subtle corn taste and is perfect with the beef, but serve mashed potatoes (potatoes mashed with celery root would be good) if you prefer. Polenta is a last-minute dish—it doesn't reheat well—but I find that it will sit for up to thirty minutes, which is about the time it takes to eat the first course. You can then add more milk and reheat, beating well to break the polenta down. If you're going to reheat it, don't add the butter and cheese until you're about to serve. Otherwise, take a break between the appetizer and the main course and chat with everyone while you stir.

serves 6

2 tablespoons regular olive oil

4–5 beef cheeks, about 3¼lb or more in total

sea salt flakes and freshly ground black pepper

2 onions, coarsely chopped

2 large carrots, finely chopped

2 celery stalks, finely chopped

2 garlic cloves, crushed

3 tablespoons Marsala or Port

1 scant cup red wine

5 cups beef stock

1 cinnamon stick

6 juniper berries, bruised

6 thyme sprigs

2 bay leaves

for the polenta

1¼ cups whole milk

1¼ cups coarse polenta (don't buy the quick-cooking variety)

⅔ stick unsalted butter

½ cup finely grated Parmesan cheese

Preheat the oven to 300°F.

Heat the regular olive oil in a large Dutch oven and brown the meat all over, seasoning it, too. Remove from the pan. Add the onions, carrots, and celery and cook over medium-low heat until the onions are pale gold and soft, about 5 minutes, stirring. Add the garlic and cook for a couple of minutes, then pour on the Marsala or Port, then the wine, and cook until reduced by half. Add the stock, spices, and herbs, and season, then return the meat to the pan. Bring to a very gentle simmer.

Cover and cook in the oven for 4 hours. Turn the beef cheeks over every so often. By the end of cooking, the meat should be melting.

Remove the meat and strain the cooking liquid. Lift the fat off the top of the cooking juices and discard (adding ice cubes will help the fat to set slightly on top, which makes this easier). Put the juices back in the pan and reduce by boiling, if you want them to be thicker. Halve each beef cheek (or cut into smaller pieces) and return to the cooking juices.

For the polenta, put the milk into a large, heavy pan with 2¾ cups of water and ¾ teaspoon sea salt flakes and bring to a boil. Add the polenta, letting it run in thin streams through your fingers, whisking continuously. Stir for 2 minutes until it thickens.

Turn the heat right down and stir every 4 to 5 minutes, to prevent the polenta from sticking, for about 40 minutes. It should be coming away from the sides of the pan. You might need to add more water; it shouldn't get dry and stiff, but should be thick and unctuous. Stir in the butter and Parmesan, taste for seasoning, then serve in a warmed bowl with the reheated beef. Cavolo nero would be perfect on the side.

bonet

Gloriously old-fashioned and a real showstopping dessert. It looks very impressive but is, in fact, extremely simple to make.

serves 6

flavorless oil, for the pan

1¼ cups granulated sugar

2 tablespoons blanched hazelnuts, lightly toasted

1¼ cups whole milk

1 cup heavy cream

1 tablespoon instant espresso powder

1½ tablespoons unsweetened cocoa powder

2¼oz dark chocolate, 70 percent cocoa solids, chopped

3 medium eggs

¼ cup superfine sugar

1 tablespoon dark rum

1½ cups crushed amaretti cookies

Preheat the oven to 340°F. Lightly oil an 8 x 4 x 2½ inch loaf pan and a baking pan, using a pastry brush or a wad of paper towels.

Make caramel: heat the granulated sugar and about ½ cup of water gently in a saucepan until the sugar has completely dissolved. You must not stir it, but you can tip the saucepan to ensure the heat reaches every bit of the bottom. Now turn up the heat and cook until the sugar turns toffee-colored and caramelizes. You will know when it's ready by the color and smell; be careful not to burn it. As soon as it reaches this point, quickly pour half into the bottom of the loaf pan. Add the hazelnuts to the other half remaining in the saucepan and pour that onto the oiled baking pan. Tilt the loaf pan to coat the bottom and some of the inside walls with the caramel. Let this set. Let the caramel on the baking pan set, too, then coarsely break it up and set aside (you'll use this for decoration later).

Put the milk and cream into a saucepan and bring to a simmer. Add the coffee powder, cocoa, and chopped chocolate and stir until the chocolate is melted, then immediately remove from the heat.

Using an electric hand mixer, beat the eggs and superfine sugar together until they form soft peaks. Slowly add the warm milk and chocolate mixture, pouring it from a height to cool it as it pours, then add the rum and crushed amaretti and mix well. Pour this into the loaf pan and stand it in a deep roasting pan. Add enough just-boiled water to come one-third to halfway up the sides of the loaf pan.

Bake for 1 hour (it may need as much as 1¼ hours). The top should feel set when you touch the center, but will still tremble slightly. Remove from the water bath and let cool. Cover the top with plastic wrap, put in the fridge, and let stand for 6 hours to firm up.

Remove the plastic wrap. Run a knife between the *bonet* and the pan, then carefully invert onto a serving plate. The caramel should run down the sides. Decorate with the hazelnuts in caramel.

missing new york

oysters and manhattans

oysters with mignonette

hanger steak with roast beets & horseradish cream

manhattan creams with citrus caramel

It's 1968 and I'm sitting on a rug in the garden. My mum is reading from one of the American books we got free with our new set of Collier's Encyclopedias. Every time she finishes the story of "Rosa Too Little" I beg her to read it again. I want it over and over. Rosa lives in a brownstone in New York and her family can't afford books (never mind a set of encyclopedias) and she's too little to join the library. Instead, she plays in the bright sprays of water that gush from the fire hydrants on hot days. By the end of the story, Rosa joins the library and can have as many books as she wants. She is Rosa Too Little no longer. I was waiting to join the library too and, because of Rosa, I knew it was going to happen. I also—because I wanted to be there, dancing in the water, then sitting on the stoop with Rosa—fell in love with New York.

I'm not the only one. New York is a nexus of lights and hope. We feel we know it even if we've never been. Irish people have always been drawn there, because of famine or poverty or simple optimism. In the early 1860s, one in every four New Yorkers was an Irish immigrant. I grew up in a different time in Irish history but I knew, early on (the Troubles started in the late 1960s), that I would have to leave Northern Ireland. Home was never really home. I was only going to be there for a little while. I played "Rhapsody in Blue"—one of only ten LPs we had—and fed my fantasy with books (a Canadian aunt sent picture-books in which children ate cookies the size of the moon and shopped in dime stores). I wanted to be in New York.

By the age of eleven, I thought I could be Rhoda Morgenstern, even though I was neither Jewish nor from the Bronx. She was just so sassy. We lived in the middle of the countryside but, at night, I would look out the landing window at the lights across the fields. It was actually the glow of the nearby housing project—and the small row of shops where we sometimes picked up groceries—but no matter. With a determined imagination and the right music it was the sparkling edges of Manhattan.

Even going to Dublin got me that bit nearer. When we went there on vacation we always visited the airport, not to fly somewhere, but to experience the *possibility* of flying somewhere. The departures board was intoxicating. "Bong bing, Aer Lingus!" my siblings and I would say, imitating the finest Dublin accent, then laugh ourselves silly. We watched the big white and green birds with shamrocks on their sides take off for Boston and Chicago and New York. You see? New York wasn't far away. But I only got there in stages. New York is a fantasy and the first few times you visit that's all you see. Walk/ Don't Walk signs, plumes of steam rising from manhole covers, skyscraper restaurants from where you can view the whole glittering grid of the city, surly bartenders who say "Whaddya want?" It's a movie made real, and you run your own narrative and images. The thing that made me happiest, on my first visit, was that the Empire State Building wasn't swanky. It was nearly Christmas and the pots of poinsettia in the lobby were covered in old crinkled aluminum foil. I thought it was exactly as it would have looked if I'd visited with Rosa in 1968.

I wanted to watch the skating at the Rockefeller Center, look down the central spine of the Guggenheim, see Jasper Johns's *Flag* at The Museum of Modern Art, but most of my plans centered around food. The hot dog carts, the red sauce Italian restaurants, the little cardboard cartons of Chinese takeout, these were as much a part of New York as the Statue of Liberty. For a long time I'd been looking at what New York chefs were cooking and I chose my restaurants carefully. Two of them—Annie Rosenzwieg's Arcadia and Danny Meyer's Union Square Café—remained favorites for years. I explored simple neighborhood joints, too. I wanted a diner I could call my own. "Can you speak Spanish?" drawled the waiter in one place (as I tried to eat a sandwich as big as my head). "Why?" "Because this dude doesn't speak English and I'm havin' trouble here." So I took the order from the man from Venezuela—feeling like a native—and understood that eating in New York wasn't just about food, but about interaction.

I returned from that first trip with a tortilla press from Zabar's (you can forget Dean & Deluca and all the fancy pants delis; I wanted to go to places that were chaotic and scuffed at the edges) and a notebook full of ideas, not for books or columns (I wasn't a food writer then), but for my own kitchen. I look to New York for shots of culinary energy. When I'm at home in London I enjoy it vicariously by checking out the menus of favorite restaurants online, and every week I wait for the "Hungry City" column in *The New York Times*. It doesn't cover smart places, but small inexpensive out-of-the way ones: an Uzbek restaurant where the *plov* is splattered with barberries and black cumin; a Mexican joint where the margaritas sting and English is understood, though not spoken. I could never eat my way round all these—even if I lived there—but the column offers vignettes and moods, a picture of the world that has washed up on New York's shore; life, through food, in the Naked City.

When I'm in New York I'm up and out of my hotel—breakfast being the first great meal of the day there—by 7.30 A.M. In late spring and summer the city smells of hot sidewalks (even better when they're hot and wet, then you can get a whiff of blossom in some neighborhoods) and food: garlicky pizza, hot sugar-dusted doughnuts, salty pretzels. Each day has a schedule: I visit cheese shops, bakeries, and tea houses, places that specialize in Indian breakfasts and Cantonese desserts. I eat oysters and steak and knock back Manhattans. I watch how much pleasure others take in food, like the Japanese man in a waterproof jacket, standing at a counter by himself eating crab in one of the city's food markets, his face creased with concentration. Odd places, such as the Italian where I can get eggs and anchovies on toast for breakfast and the best chocolate and hazelnut cake I've ever tasted, have become regular haunts. Some of the most enjoyable finds aren't planned, like the Irish bar I discovered at 3 A.M. Run by two Dubliners, it's a refuge for chefs who've just finished their shifts. The burgers aren't remarkable, but the high-energy exhaustion is. And everyone has a tale to tell, even if you can work it out without hearing it.

On every trip I make a pilgrimage to 97 Orchard Street on the Lower East Side. It's a museum, but not a place of glass cases and dead history. It's in an old tenement building where immigrants lived and the apartments—each representing a different family and era—tell the story of what they did and how they ate. I partly go there to be reminded of New York's beginnings and the people who made this city, but also because it's a good area for eating. Even though it's increasingly gentrified, you can still find the food of those who came and wanted the comfort of the flavors they'd left behind: the Germans, Italians, East European Jews, Chinese, and West Indians. You can still get bialys at Kosser's, lox at Russ & Daughters, and pastrami on rye at Katz's Deli. And you should. New York is still peopled by the rest of the world. One-third of the inhabitants were born elsewhere and half speak a language other than English at home. This means it's a compression of histories and dishes people hold onto, and which you can taste, too.

It's not only the edible history or the culinary diversity that seduces, though, it's the glamour. Restaurateurs here don't just create places to eat. Go to Minetta Tavern, a 1930s Greenwich Village relic that was buffed, restored, and re-opened in 2009. Pull back the heavy velvet curtain behind the door and you enter a complete world, a clubby, buzzing stage set filled with real people. You're Alice, falling down the rabbit hole. *The New York Times*'s restaurant critic, Pete Wells, has said that the city is brilliant at artifice; restaurateurs here are like theater producers. They're good at making the new feel old, too. Take a cab across the Brooklyn Bridge—a ride, as you look at the skylines on both sides of the Hudson, that most makes you feel fused with the city—and head for Maison Premiere, a restaurant, oyster house, and, as the owners describe it, "cocktail den." It looks pleasingly worn; laughter and noise spill onto the sidewalk. A small garden at the back is full of tumbling vines and a thousand tiny lights. It feels like New York, New Orleans, and Paris all rolled into one and has the confidence of a long-established haunt, but it's only been there since 2011. It takes a city with chutzpah to pull that off.

Small town girls, like me, lack cynicism and aren't prone to ennui. We're lucky. For us, a place like New York is a constant source of wonder: bright lights, big city. I make a note of places I see from buses and taxis. What does Papaya Dog sell, or the (open 24 hours) Alaska Food Market? What is lunch like at the God Bless Deli? What is more exciting than driving past block after block of neon signs that light up the most intriguing-looking dining destinations and wondering what stories you'll find there? I know New York isn't perfect. It's loud, it can be brash, people are too concerned with money. But it's also misrepresented. New Yorkers are frank rather than rude, friendly rather than in-your-face. A complete stranger will tell you that the novel you're reading isn't all that great; another will want to know what you paid for your purse. You can be anonymous here, but it's unlikely people will let you.

Somehow I never got the apartment where my Chinese could be delivered, where I would set my paper bag of groceries on the counter and wonder what to cook. I got waylaid by other things. But it's never too late to have a New York kitchen. Everything is possible…

oysters with mignonette

When you're my age, you think you've acquired your tastes. You might have taken years to come round to the inkiness of olives and the chocolatey bitterness of stout, but your food loves are fixed. I grew up with oysters, but had never really taken to them. I wanted to like them; why would you not want to eat something that houses pearls? Then, in one year, I made two trips to New York where they were a constant presence and cheap. Every bar had an "oyster happy hour" when they sold for a dollar each. Although aficionados scorn cooked oysters, that's what got me hooked. Perched on a stool in a seafood bar in Chelsea Market, I downed "pistols on horseback"—fried oysters wrapped in Serrano ham—and studied my raw oyster options: "medium salinity with a sweet ocean finish," "mild salinity, plump meat, buttery finish." This is how great white Burgundies are described. I wanted to taste all this butter and smoke and flintiness. I started to eat them every day and fell in love with the craggy bivalve and its plump, salty insides. Admittedly, their low price helped: I was under no pressure to love them. On the last night of my second trip that year, I went to Maison Premiere in Brooklyn, all twinkling lights, laughter, and dazzling cocktails. "Let's have the oyster platter," my friend said. "We'll eat oysters all the way from the East Coast to the West Coast, minerally flesh to rich buttery flesh." So we did. And it was heaven. Oysters belong to New York.

serves 4

24 oysters

crushed ice or rock salt, to serve

for the mignonette
⅔ cup Champagne vinegar or good-quality red wine vinegar

2 tablespoons very finely chopped shallots

2 teaspoons white peppercorns, coarsely ground

Mix everything for the mignonette in a jar, shake it, then put it in the fridge for 1 day, to allow time for the shallots to flavor the vinegar.

Make sure you have an oyster knife; *don't* try to shuck oysters with a regular kitchen knife. Rinse the oysters and throw away any that are open and don't close if you tap them against the sink. Place an oyster flat-side up on a work surface. Grip it with a dish cloth to help protect your hand, leaving the narrow hinged end exposed. Place the tip of the knife between the top and bottom shells next to the hinge. Push it into the shell, twisting and wiggling, to release the top shell. It may seem like you aren't getting there, but keep going with gentle pressure until it pops open. Try to keep the oyster level, so the delicious liquor (the briny, salty seawater) stays in the deeper bowl of the bottom shell. Wipe your knife, then release the shell completely by inserting the tip in a few other places and twisting. Keeping the oyster level, run your knife along the upper shell to cut the oyster from the top shell. Remove the top shell. Run your knife along the lower shell and gently cut the oyster free. Leave it nestled in the shell. (If you open an oyster that has a strong, sulfurous smell, throw it away. It's dead.)

Transfer each oyster in its shell to a bed of crushed ice or rock salt to keep it level, while you open the rest. Serve immediately, with the mignonette; you'll need about ¼ teaspoon for each oyster.

hanger steak with roast beets & horseradish cream

A hanger steak is usually about 1¼ inches thick and shaped like a small, fat snake. It is slightly chewy—but only *slightly*—and has a good gamey flavor. London-based chef Neil Rankin taught me how to cook steak (the instructions for all cuts are in his book, *Low and Slow*) and it works every time. Sautéed potatoes and watercress are good on the side.

serves 4

1lb 2oz small raw beets

regular olive oil

sea salt flakes and freshly ground black pepper

½ cup heavy cream

1 tablespoon wholegrain mustard, or to taste

3 tablespoons freshly grated horseradish

splash of white wine vinegar (optional)

pinch of superfine sugar (optional)

4 x 9oz hanger steaks (keep them in the fridge)

flavorless oil or rendered beef fat, for frying

Preheat the oven to 410°F.

Trim the beets and wrap in foil, moistening with a little regular olive oil and seasoning before you seal the package. Don't wrap it too tightly; you want there to be space around the beets. Place in a roasting pan and cook until tender; it should take 30 to 35 minutes, though the time can vary. Test with the point of a knife. When the beets are done the point should pass through with no resistance. When the beets are cool enough to handle, peel, quarter, and season. These can be served at room temperature.

Reduce the oven temperature to 275°F. Put in an empty roasting pan or baking pan large enough to hold all the steaks.

Whip the cream and add the mustard and horseradish and taste it; you may want a little more mustard. Some people add a tiny splash of white wine vinegar (or, conversely, a pinch of sugar). Add whichever of those you think you would like.

Hanger steaks don't have flat surfaces, so flatten each steak a bit by bashing it with the base of a saucepan, putting nonstick parchment paper over it first. Don't overdo it, you just need to make them a little less round.

Heat 2 skillets, preferably cast iron, 7 to 10 minutes ahead of when you want to cook the steaks, setting the heat dial about three-quarters of the way around. To check whether the skillet is hot enough to cook in, add a tiny amount of flavorless oil or fat. If it smokes, the skillet is ready. Heat a little oil or beef fat in the skillet, add 2 steaks to each, and press down with tongs to get the surfaces in touch with the bottom of the skillet. Move the steaks around all the time, seasoning and making sure each steak is getting browned all over. Listen for the sizzle: when the steak is quiet, you need to move it. If the pan gets too hot and the meat is getting too dark (you don't want it to be black), reduce the heat; if it's not getting dark enough, increase the heat.

Transfer the steaks to the hot baking pan in the oven and continue to cook for about 5 minutes for medium-rare (hanger steak is best served medium-rare).

Using a really sharp knife, slice each steak against the grain. Neil Rankin (see recipe introduction) doesn't rest his steak. Serve with the roast beets and the horseradish cream. A handful of salad greens are good on the side.

manhattan creams with citrus caramel

Oh, there are so many desserts that say "New York!" I struggled over the choice, juggling brownies, roast apple and bourbon ice cream, upside-down pear and cranberry tarts...but in the end I settled on this. It has the flavors of a Manhattan—bourbon, sweet vermouth, and a dash of Angostura bitters—captured in a pannacotta. You can use oranges or blood oranges instead of grapefruit, if you prefer. This is possibly the best dessert in the book...not counting the ice cream, of course. Make it often: it's classic, useful, and able to take all sorts of different adornments. It works well with roast peaches, apricots, and pears, poached plums, or caramelized slices of apples, though use orange rather than grapefruit juice for the caramel if you want to serve it with any of these fruits.

serves 4

for the cream
¼oz gelatin leaves (they can be any grade, though I use platinum)

⅔ cup whole milk

1¼ cups heavy cream

½ cup superfine sugar

squeeze of lemon juice

2 tablespoons plus 1 teaspoon bourbon

1 tablespoon sweet white vermouth

good dash of Angostura bitters

1 large red grapefruit

for the citrus caramel
1 scant cup pink grapefruit juice

3 tablespoons lemon juice

½ cup superfine sugar

You will need 4 metal molds, each with a capacity of 4 fluid ounces.

Soak the gelatin leaves in cold water for about 10 minutes; they will soften. Pour the milk and cream into a heavy saucepan with the sugar and place over low heat, stirring a little to help the sugar dissolve. Remove from the heat and let cool until hand-warm.

Lift the gelatin leaves from the water and squeeze out excess liquid. Stir into the milk and cream mixture. The mixture should not be hot: if it's too hot it will affect the gelatin's setting properties; if it is too cold, on the other hand, the gelatin won't dissolve. Add the lemon juice, bourbon, vermouth, and bitters. Pour into the metal molds and let cool, then set in a small roasting pan (this just makes things easier), cover with plastic wrap and chill to set for about 4 to 6 hours.

For the citrus caramel, mix the grapefruit and lemon juices together. Put the sugar in a heavy saucepan with ⅓ cup of water. Set over medium heat and cook, gently tipping the pan every so often, until the sugar has dissolved. Increase the heat to high and cook until caramelized: you will know by the smell and color, but be careful not to take it too far (it goes from caramelized to burned very quickly). You need to tip the pan as the sugar caramelizes around the edges, to spread the caramelization. Quickly add the citrus juices, standing well back (the caramel will bubble and spit). Stir and let simmer for about 2 minutes, then remove from the heat. Let cool completely.

Trim the top and bottom of the grapefruit (it will now have a base on which to sit). Working from top to bottom and turning the grapefruit

around as you go, remove the peel and pith (use a small sharp knife) in broad strips. Slide a small knife with a fine blade between the flesh and membrane and ease each segment out. Keep the segments as neat as possible. You should end up with 12 neat segments, 3 for each person.

To serve, dip the base of each mold into just-boiled water for a few seconds, then invert onto a plate, give the cream a shake, and allow it to slip out. Spoon some of the citrus caramel around each cream and add the grapefruit segments.

it's all about the pasta

winter treats

sparkling wine with bergamot syrup

shaved fennel, celery & apple salad with pomegranates & hazelnuts

vincisgrassi

blood orange & aperol jellies

This menu is completely built around the *vincisgrassi*, an obscure lasagne dish (some date its origins to as early as 1779) from the Marches of Italy. It's very rich, though not as rich as the original, which contained coxcombs, sweetbreads, and brains. I first ate vincisgrassi at The Walnut Tree Inn in Wales, where it was cooked by Franco Taruschio. His version featured shaved truffles and porcini. Mine is another step down the luxury scale, but you can easily add truffles and use fresh wild mushrooms if you're feeling extravagant. There are many different versions of this dish in Italian cookbooks, some more like meat lasagne (with a ragù made from veal), but all contain wild mushrooms and Parma ham. It's an exquisite dish. I tend to be quiet when I eat it, not out of reverence (though that would not be *entirely* out of place), but just because I want to savor every mouthful.

It's worth making your own pasta for the *vincisgrassi*. It needs fresh, silky sheets. And because you only have to form rectangles, you don't need to be a whiz at cutting it. If you have to buy the pasta, get the best fresh stuff you can find.

The appetizer salad is there for freshness. The dessert is simple and slightly bitter and provides a perfect ending, although a sorbet would be good too, or even just a glass of vin santo.

sparkling wine with bergamot syrup

This isn't mandatory—a cocktail made with winter blood oranges would be just as lovely—but it's hard to resist an unusual flavor and bergamots (which give Earl Grey tea its unique scent) are like nothing else. You might have trouble tracking them down, but see page 252 for possible sources. If you can't get hold of any, you can use this recipe to make a lime syrup. It won't be like a bergamot version, but you'll still be using a winter citrus fruit and making something unusual.

makes about 1 quart of
syrup

10 bergamots (or see recipe
introduction), scrubbed in warm,
soapy water

2½ cups granulated sugar

to serve

1 bottle of chilled sparkling dry
white wine

Finely grate the bergamot zest, then halve and squeeze each fruit. Put the zest into a saucepan with the sugar and 2 cups of water. Slowly bring to a boil, stirring to help the sugar dissolve. Reduce the heat and simmer for 5 minutes, then remove from the heat and add the juice. Return to a simmer and cook for 2 minutes, then let cool. Strain through a sieve lined with cheesecloth then pour through a funnel into a sterilized bottle (see page 86).

To serve, put a little of the syrup into each glass—don't use too much as the bergamot flavor is strong—and top off with the sparkling wine.

shaved fennel, celery & apple salad with pomegranates & hazelnuts

This might seem very humble before a resplendent pasta dish, but that's the point. It's clean and plain and a real appetite opener. Don't make it too far in advance, though, as the fennel and apples lose their freshness.

serves 6

2 small fennel bulbs

2 small eating apples

juice of 1 lemon

2 celery stalks, with leaves if possible, washed and trimmed

⅓ cup extra virgin olive oil

1 tablespoon white balsamic vinegar

¼ teaspoon Dijon mustard

sea salt flakes and freshly ground black pepper

seeds from ½ pomegranate

2 tablespoons halved hazelnuts, toasted

Quarter the fennel, trim the tops and the bases, and remove any coarse outer leaves. If there are any little fronds, remove and reserve them. Quarter and core the apples. Don't leave any of this sitting around to discolor: prepare and assemble the salad quickly.

Using a mandoline slicer—or a very sharp, thin-bladed knife—slice the fennel very thinly and put it into a large bowl with the lemon juice. Slice the celery finely on an angle, reserving any leaves. Change the setting on your mandoline slicer and slice the apples into slightly thicker pieces. Toss the celery and apples in the lemon juice, too. Add any fennel fronds and celery leaves you reserved.

Mix the extra virgin olive oil with the white balsamic vinegar, mustard, and salt and pepper. Add this to the bowl, mixing it with the other contents. Taste the salad for seasoning. Just before serving, scatter with the pomegranate seeds and hazelnuts.

vincisgrassi

This—like an indulgent, bosky lasagne—is one of my favorite dishes in the world. When Franco Taruschio was chef-owner of the Walnut Tree Inn in Abergavenny, I used to go there just to eat it. This is based on his recipe, though I don't use truffles as he does because I think this dish is rich enough without them. But if you're in the money, then add shaved white truffle. Likewise, use fresh wild mushrooms if you can afford them. I have to confess I stopped making pasta very often after I had children, but every time I do, I think it's worth the effort. The pasta here is fine and light; you don't so much eat it as allow it to slip down.

serves 6

for the pasta

2 whole medium eggs and 4 egg yolks

2 to 2¼ cups Italian type "oo" flour, plus more to dust

1 teaspoon sea salt flakes

1lb fresh mushrooms, divided

1oz dried wild mushrooms

2 tablespoons unsalted butter, divided, plus more for the dish

regular olive oil

sea salt flakes and freshly ground black pepper

2 tablespoons finely chopped flat-leaf parsley leaves

1oz prosciutto, torn

1½ cups grated Parmesan cheese, plus more to serve

truffle oil, to serve (optional)

for the béchamel

5 cups whole milk

½ onion

2 bay leaves

8 black peppercorns

3½ tablespoons unsalted butter

⅔ cup all-purpose flour

1 scant cup heavy cream

Lightly beat the 2 whole eggs and keep the 4 yolks nearby in a separate bowl. Put the flour into another bowl and sprinkle on the salt. Make a well in the center of the flour and add the whole eggs. Bring the flour into the well with your hands, mixing it with the eggs. Gradually add the yolks, until the dough forms a ball. Put the dough onto a lightly floured surface and knead for 6 minutes. It should be smooth and slightly elastic. Seal in plastic wrap and chill for 1 hour.

Slice the fresh mushrooms. Put the dried mushrooms in a bowl and cover with boiling water. Melt one-third to half the butter in a skillet, add ½ tablespoon regular olive oil, and sauté one-third to half the fresh mushrooms, depending on the size of your pan (it shouldn't be overcrowded or the mushrooms will stew rather than sauté), seasoning well. They should take on some color, and the liquid they exude should evaporate. Remove to a large bowl, add more butter and oil to the pan and repeat, to sauté all the fresh mushrooms. Drain the dried mushrooms and add to the last batch of fried mushrooms with the parsley. Mix in the ham as well.

Now make the béchamel. Heat the milk with the onion, bay leaves, and peppercorns until boiling. Remove from the heat and leave to infuse for 30 minutes. Strain. Melt the butter in a heavy saucepan, add the flour, and blend well. Cook for 2 minutes, then take off the heat and add a small drop of milk, beating well to prevent lumps, then gradually add all the milk. Return to the heat and bring to a boil, stirring. The mixture will thicken. Simmer for 3 minutes. Stir in the cream, then the mushroom mixture. Heat gently and season to taste.

Lightly flour your table. Cut the dough into 3. Set your pasta machine to its widest opening. Shape the first piece of dough to fit the machine

and feed it through 4 times, turning and folding it each time. Continue, adjusting the width of the opening by moving down one setting at a time, with all the dough. Put each sheet of pasta on the floured table. Cut into 5-inch squares.

Preheat the oven to 400°F. Butter a 12 x 8 inch ovenproof dish. Bring a large saucepan of salted water to a boil. Cook 4 squares of pasta at a time, transferring them immediately to a large bowl of cold water to stop them cooking. Drain them as you go and lay them on dish cloths, blotting them dry.

Assemble the *vincisgrassi*, starting with a layer of pasta, then sauce, a sprinkling of Parmesan, and so on, ending with a layer of sauce, then Parmesan. Bake for 20 to 30 minutes. Drizzle with truffle oil, if you like. Serve with a bowl of Parmesan.

blood orange & aperol jellies

You need something "clean" and uncluttered after a main course such as *vincisgrassi*. Even though it's winter, a sorbet would also be good, or just finish with a big bowl of grapes or blood oranges. I especially like a jelly. This is not jello, but a proper jelly made with gelatin; it may seem like a lot of gelatin but that's because alcohol inhibits its setting properties. This dessert has a pleasing bitterness because of the Aperol. Bitterness provides a good full-stop after richness.

serves 6

for the gelatin

1 cup Aperol

1¾ cups prosecco

⅔ cup freshly squeezed blood orange juice, plus 3 broad strips of the zest

1 tablespoon granulated sugar

⅔oz gelatin leaves (they can be any grade, though I use platinum as it gives a clearer jelly)

1 tablespoon lemon juice

5 small blood oranges, or sweet oranges, segmented (see page 216–217)

for the cream

confectioners' sugar, to taste

½ teaspoon vanilla extract

1 cup mascarpone

Put the Aperol, prosecco, orange juice, zest, and sugar in a saucepan and bring to just below a boil, stirring occasionally to help the sugar dissolve. Reduce the heat to very low and simmer for about 5 minutes. Meanwhile, soak the gelatin in a small bowl of cold water for about 3 minutes to soften.

Strain the boozy mixture into a small pitcher. Gently squeeze any excess water out of the softened gelatin and stir it into the warm (not hot or boiling) liquid until it dissolves. Add the lemon juice.

Divide one-third of the liquid among 6 glasses. Let cool, then refrigerate to set. Once they have a fairly firm surface, divide half the orange segments among the glasses and gently reheat the remaining gelatin mixture to render it liquid once more (you should always be able to put your finger into it; too much heat will destroy the gelatin's setting properties). Let cool a little and top off the glasses evenly with half the liquid. Refrigerate to set.

Repeat with the remaining segments and liquid gelatin, then refrigerate for 4 hours, or as long as it takes to set.

Beat the confectioners' sugar and vanilla into the mascarpone. Top each serving with a swirl of the mascarpone cream, or offer it on the side.

a lunch to soothe

especially for Saturdays

jambon cru on sourdough with bitter greens

smoked haddock & celery root gratin

rhubarb, marmalade & rosemary cake

I'm a big fan of the Saturday lunch. It's easier to pull off than Sunday lunch—there is no pressure to have a roast with all the concurrent anxiety about the "rise" on your Yorkshire pudding—and it's more relaxed for other reasons, too. The weekend is only halfway through, rather than near its end, and you can finish lunch and still go out for the evening. Lunch *and* the cinema. Optimism reigns…

A Saturday lunch in winter demands a certain kind of dish, though: sausages and mashed potatoes; fish pie; gratins; big, easy pasta dishes. You want the familiar, food you can eat with just a fork, the soothing richness of cream. Nothing should be grand; people need to relax, read the paper, get their own drinks.

The appetizer here is pretty much thrown together; you only have to make a vinaigrette with shallots, toast bread, wash greens. Shove the main course gratin in the oven and let it take care of itself. The cake requires a little effort (nearly all cakes do) and really ought to be made the day before. Baked stuffed apples, pears poached in red wine or baked in Marsala are good alternatives. And, if you want to make life really easy, stew some apples. I never refuse applesauce, and I'm not sure why people don't have the confidence to serve it for dessert more often. Because of the cream in the gratin, though, you can't really fall back on those other obvious weekend desserts, such as bread-and-butter pudding or baked rice pudding, as they would make the meal too rich. Cheese with ripe pears or apples and nuts would be perfect, though, and Epoisses, Comté, Morbier, and Cheddar are all good in winter.

Kirs are for summer. In the colder months, a communard—a drop of cassis topped off with red wine, rather than white—is lovely before this meal. Or make some mulled hard cider, especially if it's cold. I don't think mulled drinks should be saved just for Christmas.

jambon cru on sourdough with bitter greens

I'm very fond of the "little something on bread" appetizer; in fact, I had to stop myself from putting too many in this book. They're easy and the bread provides a base for strong flavors. Use slices of sourdough that aren't too big—it's just an appetizer after all, and you do have a starchy main course to come—and buy a proper curly endive lettuce (frisée)—pre-bagged lettuce tastes of nothing. You won't use all of it, so keep the rest for another meal. The bitterness of the leaves against the fattiness of the ham is the point here. I am not ordinarily a weigher of chopped shallots. However, I wanted to be specific about the amount I use in this dressing because if you added a whole large banana shallot, for instance, it would be way too thick.

serves 8

1 curly endive (frisée)

8 slices of sourdough bread, not too big and not too thick

16 slices of *jambon de Bayonne*, prosciutto, or Serrano ham

for the dressing
2 tablespoons white wine vinegar

1½ teaspoons Dijon mustard

sea salt flakes and freshly ground black pepper

⅔ to ¾ cup extra virgin olive oil (a fruity rather than a grassy one)

good pinch of superfine sugar (optional)

¼ cup very finely chopped shallots

First make the dressing. Put the vinegar, mustard, and seasoning into a small bowl and whisk in the extra virgin olive oil with a fork. The mixture should emulsify. Don't add all the oil at once; always taste it as you go, as the amount you add depends on the acidity of the vinegar you've used and even on the Dijon mustard, so adjust (and tweak the seasoning, too, if you need to). I always add a pinch of sugar as well. You can keep any dressing you don't use. Add the shallots to this and let it sit for a while; they soften and also flavor the vinaigrette.

Concentrate on the paler green and yellow inner leaves of the curly endive (frisée). (The coarse outer leaves can be used for soup; they make a good potato and bitter greens soup with lots of extra virgin olive oil and garlic.) Remove enough of the smaller leaves to provide a small salad for each serving. Wash the leaves and gently pat dry with a dish cloth.

Toast the bread on both sides. Spoon some of the dressing and shallots onto each slice: be generous, but don't use it all because you need some for the greens. The dressing should soak into the bread a little. Toss the greens with some more of the dressing. Top each slice of toast with some greens (they can tumble off the edges) and furls of ham. Grind on some black pepper and serve.

smoked haddock & celery root gratin

Smoky, rich, simple, practically no dishes to do. If you don't want to use celery root (which is quite herbal), you can make this with potato only, or a mixture of potato and Jerusalem artichoke, which will give a sweeter result. A green vegetable—broccoli, cabbage, or salad greens—is all you need on the side.

serves 8

3 medium to large leeks

2½ tablespoons unsalted butter

1½lb celery root

7oz potatoes

½ cup fish stock (chicken stock is fine, but fish stock is better)

1¼ cups heavy cream

13oz smoked haddock (Finnan haddie) fillets, skinned

sea salt flakes and freshly ground black pepper

Preheat the oven to 400°F.

Trim the tops and root ends from the leeks and remove any discolored outer layers. Slice, wash, and put into a heavy saucepan or skillet with the butter. Heat until the butter has melted, then add a splash of water, reduce the heat to low, cover, and sweat the leeks until completely soft, about 20 minutes. Check every so often to make sure they are not sticking to the bottom of the pan.

Meanwhile, peel and finely slice the celery root and potatoes: a mandoline slicer is the best tool to use, if you have one. Put the vegetable slices into a saucepan with a broad, heavy bottom, add the stock and cream, and bring to a boil. Immediately reduce the heat so the mixture is gently simmering, then allow to cook for 15 minutes.

Cut the fish into slices about 1½ inches wide.

Put half the celery root mixture into a gratin or pie dish, seasoning as you go (not too much salt because of the smoked haddock). Add half the leeks, then all the smoked haddock, then the rest of the leeks, then the other half of the celery root and potatoes.

Bake in the oven for 30 minutes, until the gratin is tender within and golden on top. Serve immediately with a green vegetable, or a salad of watercress or chicory.

rhubarb, marmalade & rosemary cake

I love the way that flavors interconnect. Citrus fruits are good with the resinous flavor of rosemary (I adore rosemary in marmalade, both orange and grapefruit). Marmalade and rhubarb are good together in a bread-and-butter pudding. Could rhubarb also work with rosemary? It does. In this, all three ingredients are brought together.

serves 8 to 10

2 sticks unsalted butter, softened, plus more for the pan

2 cups superfine sugar

8 rosemary sprigs

1¼ cups ground almonds

3 large eggs, at room temperature, lightly beaten

⅔ cup marmalade, plus 2 tablespoons for the glaze

finely grated zest of 1 orange

¾ cup all-purpose flour

¾ cup polenta

1 teaspoon baking powder

sea salt flakes

10½oz rhubarb, trimmed and cut into pieces 1¼ inches long

2 tablespoons granulated sugar

Preheat the oven to 325°F. Butter an 8-inch springform cake pan and line the bottom with nonstick parchment paper.

Put the sugar and 2 of the rosemary sprigs into a mortar and bash with a pestle for a couple of minutes, to help the rosemary infuse the sugar. Remove the sprigs, shaking off the sugar, and discard them.

Beat the butter and rosemary sugar together until pale and fluffy. Stir in the ground almonds, then beat the eggs in a little at a time, mixing well after each addition.

Fold in the marmalade, orange zest, flour, polenta, baking powder, and a pinch of salt.

Lay 3 rosemary sprigs in the bottom of the prepared pan. Spoon in the batter and lay the rest of the rosemary on top.

Toss the rhubarb with the granulated sugar, then spread this on top. Bake for 1 hour 20 minutes, or until a skewer inserted into the middle comes out clean. (You will need to cover the cake with foil in the last 20 minutes, as it can get quite dark.)

Gently heat the extra 2 tablespoons of marmalade in a saucepan until it becomes syrupy (help to break it down by pressing with the back of a spoon), then push it through a sieve to remove any bits of zest. Let it set a little, just enough to make it easily spreadable, then, using a pastry brush, brush the marmalade glaze thickly on top of the cake.

Let cool, then run a knife between the cake and its pan, and carefully remove the cake, then the base of the pan and the baking parchment. Slide the cake onto a plate to serve.

midnight at the oasis

a middle eastern feast

moroccan-spiced quick pickles | semolina bread with orange & aniseed

olive-oil braised leeks with harissa & dill | pumpkin with *shatta* & black barley

roast broccolini with chile, feta & preserved lemon yogurt

fennel, cucumber & grape salad with pistachios

hibiscus poached pears

Middle Eastern and North African food is great for dark winter days. It gives a jolt to your tastebuds and the spread of dishes can look lavish. Start this meal with the pickles and bread, adding hard-boiled eggs and little dishes of preserved lemons, harissa (loosened with a little olive oil and water), tahini, date syrup, olives, and Greek yogurt. Offer raki to drink. Then you just need to bring on the other savory dishes, once everyone has nibbled at the appetizers. Don't bother clearing up. It will feel like a feast.

This menu, quite by accident, is vegetarian (and I don't think anyone will miss meat or fish) but you could add spiced roast chicken or lamb—keep it simple, as the vegetable dishes have a lot going on in them—if you want. Buy Arab flatbread (serve it warm) and skip making dessert, just offering bought Middle Eastern pastries for dessert, if you want to make things easier.

moroccan-spiced quick pickles

These are not proper pickles but refrigerator pickles. They won't last longer than a couple of weeks in the fridge, as the vegetables haven't been salted, but if you're going to eat them quickly, why go to all the trouble of salting? If you use radishes and red onions they give the liquid a lovely pink color.

fills a 2-quart jar

1¾lb vegetables: peeled carrots, red onion, white cabbage, cauliflower florets, radishes

1 tablespoon caraway seeds

2 teaspoons black peppercorns

½ tablespoon coriander seeds

3¼ cups white wine vinegar

¼ cup granulated sugar

1 tablespoon sea salt flakes

2 thyme sprigs

1 tablespoon crushed red pepper

6 garlic cloves, very finely sliced

optional
extra virgin olive oil; harissa; chopped dill; preserved lemons, seeded, and chopped

Slice the carrots into disks or slim batons. Peel, halve, and slice the onion into slim wedges, cut the cabbage into chunks, and slice the biggest cauliflower florets into 3 (leave small florets as they are). Trim and wash the radishes thoroughly, then slice them in half lengthwise. Put the vegetables into a large bowl. Put the caraway seeds, peppercorns, and coriander seeds in a mortar and bruise them with the pestle.

Put the vinegar and 2 cups of water into a saucepan and bring to a boil with the sugar, salt, thyme, bruised spices, crushed red pepper, and garlic. Let cool. Pour the vinegar solution over the vegetables and cover with a cloth. Let stand at room temperature for 2 days, then pack into a sterilized jar (see page 86), put in the fridge, and eat within 2 weeks.

You can alter the character of these pickles before serving. You can, of course, serve them as they are, or you can mix bowlfuls of the vegetables—in some of their vinegar—with a few tablespoons of extra virgin olive oil, some harissa, chopped dill, and perhaps some preserved lemon. Do this the day before you want to serve them. It gives a nice, oily alternative to more sharp, clean-tasting pickles.

semolina bread with orange & aniseed

I don't often make bread when I'm having guests, unless it's a very easy recipe (such as soda bread), as there's enough else to do. But with a menu where there are little dishes, and things to dip it into, bread has more of a starring role. You could just make (or buy) regular Arab flatbread to serve with this meal, but I like the slight sweetness and perfume of this loaf. It's very simple to make and has a lovely crunchy top crust, too.

makes 1 medium round loaf

2 teaspoons active dry yeast

1 teaspoon superfine sugar, divided

1¼ cups warm water

2 cups white bread flour

1½ cups semolina flour (fine ground semolina), plus more to dust (optional)

3½ tablespoons unsalted butter, melted and cooled

1½ teaspoons sea salt flakes

1½ tablespoons aniseeds, lightly bruised in a mortar

finely grated zest of 2 oranges

a little flavorless oil

a little polenta

½ tablespoon sesame seeds

Stir the yeast with ½ teaspoon of the sugar and ½ cup of the warm water in a bowl. Let stand somewhere warm for 15 minutes. The mixture will foam.

Sift the flour and semolina into a large bowl. Add the yeast mixture and half of the remaining water and start to mix everything together with your hands. Add the butter, the remaining sugar, the salt, aniseed, and orange zest. Use enough of the remaining water to make a dough.

Knead—in a mixer with a dough hook if you don't want to do it by hand—until you have a lovely elastic dough. Put this in a lightly oiled bowl, turn to coat the bread with a film of oil, then cover with plastic wrap and let stand somewhere warm until it has doubled in size (it will take about 1½ hours).

Sprinkle some polenta onto a baking sheet. Punch down the dough, form it into a ball again, then flatten this to form a disk about 10 inches across. Lay it on the prepared sheet. You can dust it with some semolina or leave it plain.

Let stand for 30 minutes, covered lightly with plastic wrap. Preheat the oven to 400°F.

Sprinkle with the sesame seeds and bake for 20 minutes, or until the top is pale brown. Let cool a little, then serve the bread warm or at room temperature.

olive oil-braised leeks with harissa & dill

You can serve this hot or at room temperature, and it tastes even better if you make it the day before. If you're making it in advance, don't add the dill until 15 minutes or so before serving, so it doesn't discolor or wilt, and make sure to take the dish out of the fridge so that it isn't cold.

serves 8

8 medium leeks

½ cup extra virgin olive oil, plus more to serve (optional)

10½oz baby waxy potatoes, peeled and sliced

5 garlic cloves, finely sliced

1¼-inch piece fresh ginger root, peeled and finely grated

1 tablespoon harissa

1¼ cups vegetable stock or water, plus more if needed

1 cup chopped pitted green olives

sea salt flakes and freshly ground black pepper

4 preserved lemons, chopped, seeds discarded

generous bunch of dill, leaves chopped

Cut off the coarse green leaves from the top of the leeks (you can use them for soup or stock) and trim the bases as well. If the outside layers look discolored, remove them, too. Cut into pieces ⅔ inch long and wash thoroughly.

Heat the extra virgin olive oil in a sauté pan and gently sauté the potatoes and leeks until they are pale gold—you really don't want to get much color on them—and the potatoes are beginning to soften. Add the garlic and ginger and sauté for another 2 minutes, then add the harissa and the stock or water. Bring to a simmer and cook, covered, until the potatoes are completely soft. Keep an eye on the level of liquid; it should reduce, but you don't want the pan to become dry or the vegetables to burn.

Add the olives, season, and cook for another 3 minutes or so. If the dish has too much liquid, leave the lid off and allow it to evaporate; if it is dry, add a little stock or water. You should end up with the leeks and potatoes just coated in oil and harissa. You might want to add a little extra virgin olive oil. Taste for seasoning and stir in the preserved lemons and dill.

pumpkin with *shatta* & black barley

Shatta is a Middle Eastern sauce. I've seen it called "red zhug," but it really tastes very different to the green Yemeni zhug that I know. It's sweeter, less herby, not so hot. Don't be put off by the large amount of tomato paste; it works. *Shatta* goes with masses of dishes—try it spooned over vegetables, or with kebabs and pilafs—but is best tempered with yogurt. Black barley isn't easy to find, but looks great—a glossy deep, dark purple—and tastes robust and nutty. If you can't find it, use hulled barley (its outer casing is hulled, not removed as in pearl barley). Don't use pearl barley, it doesn't have the structure or nuttiness you need.

serves 8

for the shatta

10 red chiles, halved, 8 seeded, all coarsely chopped

6 garlic cloves, coarsely chopped

½ cup extra virgin olive oil

⅓ cup tomato paste

1½ teaspoons ground cumin

juice of ½ lemon

1oz each cilantro and flat-leaf parsley leaves, chopped

for the pumpkin

3½lb pumpkin

⅓ cup regular olive oil

1 tablespoon unsalted butter

1 teaspoon fennel seeds

1¼-inch piece ginger root, grated

3 garlic cloves, very finely sliced

for the barley

2 teaspoons unsalted butter

1 tablespoon regular olive oil

4 shallots, finely chopped

1⅓ cups black barley, rinsed

⅓ cup dry white vermouth

3 cups chicken or vegetable stock

2 bay leaves

To make the *shatta*, put everything, except the herbs, into a food processor with ½ cup of water and, using the pulse button, whiz to a chunky purée. Add the herbs and, again using the pulse button, blend until you have a purée flecked with green (it's better if the *shatta* isn't completely blended, as the color turns quite khaki).

Preheat the oven to 375°F. Halve the pumpkin and scoop out and discard the seeds and fibers. Cut into slices about 1¼ inch thick and peel each one (the skin does become soft enough to eat, but I prefer them peeled). Put the regular olive oil and butter into a roasting pan and heat gently. Add the pumpkin and season well. With your hands, rub the fat and seasoning all over the pumpkin. Roast for 20 minutes. Bruise the fennel seeds in a mortar and pestle. Take the pan out of the oven and add the fennel, ginger, and garlic, rubbing it into the pumpkin. Return to the oven and cook for another 20 minutes, or until the pumpkin is tender and slightly caramelized at the edges.

Meanwhile, cook the barley. Heat the butter and regular olive oil in a large saucepan and sauté the shallots until soft but not colored. Add the barley, turn it over in the fat, and cook for 2 minutes. Add the vermouth and cook until reduced by half, then pour in the stock, add the bay leaves, salt, and pepper. Bring to a boil, reduce the heat to medium-low, and simmer for about 40 minutes, or until tender (it still retains a little "bite" in the center of each grain) and the stock has been absorbed. Remove the bay leaves and check the seasoning (though remember you are going to serve a strongly flavored sauce with this).

Arrange the barley in a warmed broad, shallow bowl or large platter and set the pumpkin on top. Either spoon some *shatta* over, or serve it all on the side. Offer a big bowl of Greek yogurt, too.

roast broccolini with chile, feta & preserved lemon yogurt

A dish of contrasts: salty, fresh, charred, hot, and cold. Be careful to keep an eye on the broccoli, so that it doesn't become too shriveled in the oven.

serves 8

1lb 2oz broccolini

2 tablespoons regular olive oil

2 red chiles, halved, seeded, and finely chopped, divided

sea salt flakes and freshly ground black pepper

1 preserved lemon, plus 1 tablespoon of its juice

⅓ cup Greek yogurt

1 garlic clove, finely grated

1½ tablespoons crumbled feta cheese

extra virgin olive oil

Preheat the oven to 400°F.

If any of the broccoli spears have wider stalks than the rest, split them along their lengths. Put them all into a roasting pan in which the broccoli can lie in a single layer and add the regular olive oil, half the chile, and some seasoning. Toss with your hands. Put into the hot oven and roast for 15 minutes, turning the vegetables over halfway through. The broccoli should be tender and slightly charred.

Meanwhile, chop the preserved lemon flesh and rind and stir it into the yogurt with the garlic and the juice from the preserved lemon jar.

Lay the cooked broccoli on a platter, scatter the feta on top, spoon on most of the yogurt (serve the rest on the side), scatter with the remaining chile, and splash with extra virgin olive oil. Serve.

fennel, cucumber & grape salad with pistachios

The aniseed crunch of fennel is much-needed in this menu. Don't keep this just for serving with Middle Eastern menus, though, as it's also excellent with roast pork and cheese. Make the salad close to when you want to serve it, otherwise the fennel becomes tired.

serves 8

for the dressing
1 garlic clove, finely grated

2 tablespoons white balsamic vinegar

⅓ cup extra virgin olive oil

Make the dressing by whisking everything together with a fork, seasoning well with sea salt flakes and freshly ground black pepper.

Trim the tips of the fennel bulb, retaining any feathery fronds, and remove the tough outer leaves. Quarter the bulb and remove the core (don't take away too much, or the wedges will fall apart). Using a mandoline slicer, or a very sharp knife, cut the fennel into thin slices, tossing them immediately into the lemon juice in a bowl, otherwise they'll discolor.

for the salad

1 large fennel bulb

juice of 1 lemon

1 cucumber

½ red onion, shaved or very finely sliced

1 cup sliced lengthwise seedless grapes

2 tablespoons shelled unsalted pistachio nuts, chopped

20 mint leaves, torn

You can peel the cucumber if you want (not everyone can digest the skin) but I generally don't. Cut it in half lengthwise and, just as with the fennel, cut into long, slim slices, using either a sharp knife or a mandoline slicer.

Toss everything together with the dressing—including any feathery fronds of fennel you reserved—and serve.

hibiscus poached pears

Dried hibiscus flowers are used in Mexico to make hibiscus *agua fresca*—a gorgeous citrussy summer drink—but they're also used in the Middle East and I thought that the hibiscus drink, a little adapted, would be good for poaching pears. These are the deepest, craziest crimson color. You could add other flavorings—rosemary, cinnamon, ginger, or bay—but I like the pears just with hibiscus and citrus juice.

serves 8

1½oz dried hibiscus flowers

4 broad strips of lime zest

1¼ cups granulated sugar

juice of 2 limes, plus more to taste

8 pears

crème fraîche, to serve

Put the flowers in a saucepan with 3½ cups of water, the lime zest strips, and sugar. Bring to a boil. Reduce the heat and simmer gently for about 15 minutes, stirring to help the sugar dissolve. Let cool.

Pour the mixture through a sieve, pressing on the flowers to extract as much flavor as possible. Add the lime juice to the hibiscus-infused liquid. Pour this into a broad saucepan, or a sauté pan with a lid, in which the pears can lie in a single layer. Peel the pears, but leave their stalks on.

Heat the liquid to simmering and add the pears; they should be just covered so, if there isn't enough, add a little more water. Put some nonstick parchment paper on top (cut it to fit your pan) and cover with the lid. How long you need to cook the pears depends on how ripe they are: it could take 10 minutes, it could take 20. Check by piercing the flesh with the tip of knife; it should be tender. You also need to turn the pears over during cooking, otherwise one side gets darker than the other.

Lift the tender pears from the liquid with a slotted spoon and set them onto a tray where they aren't touching (if they touch each other they will continue to cook in the residual heat and might become too soft). Boil the poaching liquid until you have about 1½ cups left. Check for a balance of sweetness and citrussy-ness. You might want to add a little more lime juice. Let cool completely.

Return the pears to the cooled liquid and let stand overnight. The longer the fruits sit in it, the more they will become stained and flavored with the hibiscus syrup. Serve with slightly sweetened crème fraîche.

drunk on olive oil

because there's nothing better to be drunk on

crostini with lardo, chestnuts & truffle honey

tonno del chianti

white beans with red onions, parsley & lemon

chocolate & olive oil cake

This is a luscious meal partly because olive oil and honey both have weight—even just visualizing them being poured makes your shoulders drop—but also because there's a lot of softness: fudgy chestnuts, melting lardo, pork you could eat with a spoon, tender beans. It also seems like a luxurious meal, even though nothing in it—apart from the truffle honey—is what you might call a luxury food. Again, this is to do with the unctuousness of the olive oil.

Surprisingly, it's one of the easiest menus in the book as well. The appetizer just requires you to go shopping; the main course needs only patience; there's nothing difficult about the dessert (the cake sinks, but it's supposed to, and its center is forgiving if you slightly undercook it). There are no endless side dishes. You could add another vegetable—broccolini would be perfect—but nothing starchy. However, you may have to hold your nerve with the pork: it poaches in a lot of olive oil. You might feel anxious, as you look at this hunk of meat bathing in fat, that it won't turn into much, but it does. It's "less is more" cooking, a dish in which ingredients are transformed, but not really because of you.

The olive oil you use for the beans should be particularly good. This is the time to use a single estate extra virgin from a producer you really like. The weightiness of olive oil runs through the meal, so the flavor of your particular choice—whether grassy or buttery or fruity—is central, too.

crostini with lardo, chestnuts & truffle honey

Some dishes are an almost wicked fantasy. I give you lardo (yes, it is pure fat that has been cured, and yes, you're allowed to eat it), chestnuts that have been warmed in honey imbued with shavings of truffle (food snobs sneer at truffle honey, but I love the mixture of sweetness and boskiness), and slightly garlicky toast. A glorious little feast.

serves 8

16 to 24 thin slices of ciabatta

1 to 2 peeled garlic cloves, halved

extra virgin olive oil (mellow and fruity, not a grassy one)

1 cup white truffle honey

1½ cups cooked chestnuts (I think frozen are better than vacuum-packed)

24 very thin slices of lardo

Preheat the oven to 400°F.

Put the slices of ciabatta on cookie sheets and bake for 10 minutes. The bread should be pale gold; you don't have to turn the pieces over. Rub a cut garlic clove on each piece of the toasted bread. Drizzle with a really good extra virgin olive oil.

Gently heat the honey—it shouldn't boil—in a saucepan with the chestnuts. You want the mixture to be just warm. Serve the chestnuts in the pan in which they were warmed, with the crostini and the lardo. Let everyone help themselves.

tonno del chianti

Not tuna at all, but pork, this dish got its name because the pork—once it's cooked and is lying in its bath of olive oil—looks like tuna. It was served at the thirtieth birthday party of the great Californian restaurant Chez Panisse and is stunning, though it requires very little preparation. Use the leftover oil for frying pork or potatoes, or pouring onto white beans; it has a fantastic flavor.

serves 8

2¾lb boned shoulder of pork, fat left on but skin removed

sea salt flakes and freshly ground black pepper

4 bay leaves

4 rosemary sprigs

3 garlic bulbs, halved horizontally

2 lemons, quartered lengthwise

⅓ cup white wine

40fl oz (5 cups) regular olive oil

Preheat the oven to 300°F. Cut the pork into 3 equal pieces. Season them well all over, then place in a heavy ovenproof saucepan with the bay leaves, rosemary, garlic, lemons, and wine. Pour on the regular olive oil; the level of the oil should be about ¾ inch above the pork.

Place over a medium-low heat until you can see that the oil is just shimmering. It will take 10 to 15 minutes. Cover the pan tightly and transfer to the oven.

Cook for 2 to 2½ hours, or until the meat is meltingly tender (test it with a fork). Take out the bay leaves, rosemary, garlic, and lemons and set the bay leaves, garlic, and lemons aside for later. The garlic is delicious (guests may fight over it), while the bay leaves and lemons look lovely, and I like eating slivers of the lemons with the pork. Discard the rosemary.

Pour the olive oil into a glass measuring cup and leave it to settle. Remove most of the oil with a ladle, leaving the darker-colored cooking juices and about 1½ inches of the oil behind. It may seem strange, but the mixture of meat juices and oil makes a fantastic "gravy," delicious poured over the beans (see recipe on page 249) as well as the pork.

Serve the pork on a warmed platter with the bay leaves, garlic, and lemons. Offer the cooking juices in a sauceboat alongside. You don't so much carve this meat as pull it apart. Serve with the white beans on page 249.

white beans with red onions, parsley & lemon

Cooking your own beans gives a much more unctuous result than using the canned type; they're richer, and have a better flavor as well. Be careful not to take them too far in the cooking, though...beans that are falling apart won't work well with the wilting arugula. If you don't like arugula, use baby spinach, which will behave in a similar way. Make sure to season this dish well, as beans need it.

serves 8

2¼ cups dried cannellini beans

6 garlic cloves, peeled but left whole, plus 3 garlic cloves, finely chopped

1 onion, quartered

2 celery stalks (and a few leaves), halved

3 rosemary sprigs

3 small dried chiles

some bits of unsmoked bacon fat or pork belly, if you have it

⅓ cup regular olive oil (preferably the oil from cooking the pork, see page 247), divided

2 red onions, finely sliced

sea salt flakes and freshly ground black pepper

4½oz arugula

juice of ½ lemon

1 tablespoon finely chopped flat-leaf parsley leaves

very good-quality extra virgin olive oil, to serve

Put the beans in a large bowl and add enough water to cover them generously (they will expand). Let soak overnight.

Drain and rinse the beans and put them in a large, heavy saucepan. Add enough water to cover them by about 1½ inches. Add the whole garlic cloves, quartered onion, celery, rosemary, chiles, and bacon fat (if using) and bring to a boil, skimming off any scum that rises to the surface. Reduce the heat to a simmer and continue to cook the beans until they are tender. Add more water as you need it and keep an eye on the level; you must keep the beans covered. The cooking time will vary depending on the age of the beans; it can take anything from 45 minutes to 1½ hours.

When the beans are tender—but not collapsing—strain them; you can use the thick cooking juices in a soup. (If you're not going to serve the beans until the following day, leave them in their cooking water, as it keeps them moist.)

Heat 3 tablespoons of the regular olive oil in a large sauté pan and sauté the red onions gently until soft but not colored. Add the chopped garlic and sauté for another few minutes. Add the remaining 2 tablespoons of regular olive oil and the beans, season well, and cook until they're warm (be careful, you don't want to squash the beans and make them mushy). Toss in the arugula, lemon juice, and parsley. The arugula will wilt slightly.

Taste: beans need a lot of seasoning, so adjust it if you need to. Transfer the beans to a serving bowl, stir in some extra virgin olive oil, and serve with the pork.

chocolate & olive oil cake

It seems an odd combination, I know, but chocolate and olive oil work beautifully together. This cake has a wonderfully rich, moist center.

serves 8

unsalted butter, for the pan

7oz dark chocolate, 70 percent cocoa solids

½ cup strong-flavored extra virgin olive oil

1 cup superfine sugar, divided

2 tablespoons ground almonds or hazelnuts

pinch of sea salt flakes

5 large eggs, at room temperature, separated

confectioners' sugar, to dust (optional)

crème fraîche, to serve

Preheat the oven to 350°F, then butter an 8-inch springform cake pan and line the bottom with nonstick parchment paper. Butter seems to be gentler on the edges of cakes, whereas oil can "fry" them.

Break the chocolate into pieces and place in a heatproof bowl set over a pan of simmering water (make sure the bowl does not touch the water). Stir a little to help the chocolate to melt.

Once it's completely melted, whisk in the oil in a steady stream, then two-thirds of the superfine sugar, whisking to help the sugar dissolve in the heat of the chocolate. Remove from the heat and allow to cool a little. Stir in the ground almonds or hazelnuts, the salt, and egg yolks.

Put the egg whites into a scrupulously clean bowl with about one-third of the remaining superfine sugar. Beat with an electric hand mixer until the whites are opaque, then add another one-third of the remaining superfine sugar. Continue beating until the whites have really increased in volume, then add the last of the superfine sugar and beat until you have stiff peaks, with tips that droop slightly.

Using a really large metal spoon, loosen the chocolate mixture by folding in 1 big tablespoon of the egg whites, then fold in the rest carefully so that you don't lose too much air. Scrape the batter into the prepared pan and bake for 40 minutes. Test by inserting a fine skewer into the center of the cake. If it comes out clean, with no batter attached, the cake is ready.

Let cool in the pan; it will deflate and crack a lot, but that's fine. Carefully remove the cake from the pan and peel off the nonstick parchment paper. Put the cake onto a plate and dust with confectioners' sugar before serving, if you like. This is a chic, grown-up cake, so it needs nothing more than crème fraîche on the side.

shopping guide

There isn't an ingredient you can't find online these days and supermarkets offer a huge range of recherché foodstuffs, including items that used to be regarded as "specialized." To save on delivery costs, I generally make one order from an online company—especially from a company that has a huge range—and get lots of hard-to-find stuff all at once.

Good fruit and vegetable suppliers will usually be happy to get you unusual types, but you can also order directly from the farms in season (see right). For example, here in the UK I use Natoora, who have a great range, including bergamots, unusual Italian salad greens, top-quality winter tomatoes, and great apricots and peaches in the summer (as well as Italian cheeses and charcuterie, such as 'nduja and lardo).

Truffles are not something I order with great regularity as they're so expensive. I have listed a few online suppliers here, but you might want to ask Italian restaurants in your area about where they get theirs (if they use them). Wherever you buy them, you aren't going to get a bargain, but you want to be sure that what you buy is good.

I get all my meat (apart from ground meat) from a butcher, and all my fish at a fish market. The produce is simply better.

I rarely use Tuscan olive oils for dressings, as I find them too grassy and bitter. I prefer oils from Provence, Liguria, or Sicily. For meals where you really notice the flavor of the oil—when you're serving simple dishes such as white beans tossed with leaves, or plain roast fish, for instance—it's worth using an extra virgin olive oil from a specific producer.

Here is a list of sites to give you an idea of where to start looking for ingredients you might not be able to find locally.

ASIAN FOOD GROCER
www.asianfoodgroc.com
Online supplier of difficult-to-find ingredients and cook's tools for Japanese, Chinese, Thai, Vietnamese, and many more Asian cuisines.

CITARELLA
www.citarella.com
Fresh oysters and live blue crabs, as well as a vast range of fish and seafoods. Shipped overnight.

D'ARTAGNAN
www.dartagnan.com
Scottish partridge, as well as other meat and poultry.

GOURMET FOODSTORE
www.gourmetfoodstore.com
Burrata cheese, fresh truffles, truffle honey, 70 percent cocoa baking chocolate, nut oils, and much more.

GOURMET SWEET BOTANICALS
www.gourmetsweetbotanicals.com
Micro greens and edible flowers, harvested and shipped the same day.

KALUSTYAN'S
www.kalustyans.com
Black barley, plus flower waters, oils, and vinegars.

LA TIENDA
www.latienda.com
Spanish ingredients, including fideuá noodles, lardo, chorizo, and jamón.

PACIFIC DREAM SEAFOODS
www.pacdream.com
Live Dungeness crabs shipped overnight.

PERSIAN BASKET
www.persianbasket.com
A range of flower waters, specialty oils and vinegars, and other ingredients used in Middle Eastern cooking.

RIPE TO YOU
www.ripetoyou.com
In season, fresh bergamot, Seville and blood oranges straight from the growers in the Central San Joaquin Valley.

THE SOMERSET CIDER BRANDY COMPANY
www.ciderbrandy.co.uk
Makers of English cider and cider brandy. Contact them for a quote for overseas shipping before ordering.

SPICE JUNGLE
www.spicejungle.com
Dried cascabel and chipotle chile peppers, vanilla beans, and a huge range of unusual herbs and spices from this site.

TIMELESS NATURAL FOOD
www.timelessfood.com
Heirloom organic lentils and specialty grains.

URBANI
www.urbani.com
Fresh truffles in season, truffle honey, and truffled products.

index

acknowledgments

Books are always made by a whole group of people and I have a brilliant team. It's taken a long time to find them and I'm never letting them go. Laura Edwards, Miranda Harvey, Joss Herd, Lucy Bannell, love and thanks to you all (as ever). Thanks as well to Kendal Noctor, photographer's assistant, for making us laugh (though never making enough coffee) and to India Whiley Morton and Camilla Baynham for their boundless enthusiasm and perfectionism.

At Octopus, my publisher Denise Bates keeps an open mind, allows me to rant (even when ranting isn't really necessary), and lets me create the books I believe in. Thank you, Denise. Thanks, too, to Frances Johnson and Katherine Hockley for going the extra mile with production and for caring about the books as much as I do. Caroline Brown, you're simply the best in the business; Kevin Hawkins, keep counting.

Thanks to Fiona Beckett for various bits of advice on wine and to Rachel McCormack for keeping me on the right track with all things Catalan. John Tongue, you're the man who always can. Thank you for dealing with so many practical matters on the shoots (from building scaffolding to looking after dogs). Jenny Linford, thank you for the lovely recipe for sago *gula melaka*, the dish I couldn't stop thinking about once I'd tasted it. Oysters and manhattans to Liz Hermann, for always being such a great dining companion in NYC. Here's to many more years and many more restaurants. You're one of the reasons I'm always missing New York.

Joss, this book is for you and comes with love and thanks. I so appreciate your energy, your optimism, your kindness, and your eye for beauty. I hope you'll always be in my kitchen and my life.